The Smart Parent's Guide to Kids' TV

Milton Chen, Ph.D.

KQED
BOOKS

San Francisco

For information, address :
KQED Books & Tapes, 2601 Mariposa St., San Francisco, CA 94110.

Publisher: Pamela Byers
Editor: Sharon Epel
Research Assistant: Joni Podolsky
Book design: Sharon Smith
Production: Vicki Valentine
Illustrations: Dan Hubig
Cover Portrait: Leslie Flores

For KQED:
President & CEO: Mary G. F. Bitterman
Vice President for Publishing & New Ventures: Mark K. Powelson

Educational and nonprofit groups wishing to order this book at
attractive quantity discounts may contact KQED Books & Tapes, 2601
Mariposa St., San Francisco, CA 94110.

Library of Congress Cataloging-in-Publication Data
Chen, Milton.
        The smart parent's guide to kids' TV/Milton Chen.
        p. cm.
        Includes bibliographical references and index.
        ISBN 0-912333-47-2
        1. Television and children—United States. I. Title.
HQ784.T4C456   1994
305.23'45'083—dc20   94-20570
                                        CIP

Printing services by *Penn&Ink*
Manufactured in the United States of America
10 9 8 7 6 5 4 3 2 1

On the cover: Milton Chen, Maggie Chen, and Big Bird
Big Bird © 1994 Jim Henson Productions, Inc.

ISBN 0-912333-47-2

Distributed to the trade by Publishers Group West

The Smart Parent's Guide to Kids' TV

TABLE OF CONTENTS

ACKNOWLEDGMENTS

For several years, I have talked with my colleagues at KQED, Inc., about writing this book. After returning from a consultancy with educational media groups in South Africa in December 1993, I decided it was time to stop talking and start writing, with a little help from my friends.

Mark Powelson, Vice President of Publishing and New Ventures, recognized the need for this book early on and encouraged me to undertake the project. Pamela Byers, Publisher of Books and Tapes, brought her impressive publishing expertise to bear in shaping and marketing the book. Sharon Epel, who also serves as Editor of the *KQED Family Learning Guide*, devoted many nights and weekends editing the drafts of this book. My prose reflects her eye for organization, clarity, and the *mot juste*. Joni Podolsky of our KQED Center for Education & Lifelong Learning, herself a student of children's TV, fact-checked the manuscript and compiled and wrote the Resource List.

All four of them have been a chorus of enthusiasm and good cheer during the months it took to conceive and write this book. Due to them, it has been one of the most pleasurable experiences of my professional life.

Sandra Lopen Barker improved the manuscript through thoughtful copyediting. Sharon Smith, the book's designer, created an appealing look for the cover and interior of the book, and Dan Hubig provided the whimsical illustrations.

A number of individuals provided current materials and documentation for this book. I am grateful to John Carey of Greystone Communications, Larry Cohen of the Contra Costa County

Health Services Department, Janice Jones of the Corporation for Public Broadcasting, Donna Lloyd-Kolkin of Health and Communication Education Consultants, and David Kleeman of the American Center for Children's Television.

Several colleagues, who are also good friends, provided thoughtful and expert criticism of an initial draft. Alice Cahn of PBS, Keith Mielke of the Children's Television Workshop, Gerald Lesser of the Harvard Graduate School of Education, and Dale Kunkel from the University of California, Santa Barbara, all took time out of their busy schedules to offer insight on various points in this book.

I also express my deep gratitude and admiration to three individuals who have been an inspiration to me in my work through their conviction, compassion, and leadership in educational television. Joan Cooney, Peggy Charren, and Fred Rogers have improved the lives of American children immeasurably, and I am honored by their contributions to this book.

Finally, my wife and partner, Ruth, and our daughter, Maggie, have taught me some of the most important lessons I know about how families can use television. I've personally learned to practice what I preach: setting limits, selecting programs, and turning off the set in search of other activities. They've endured my absence during this period with good humor, even though I was just downstairs staring at the computer screen.

After seeing me hunched over so many screens of text, Maggie offered this advice: "Dad, I think your book needs some pictures." The right pictures to go with this book are on your TV. I hope this book helps you to find them.

FOREWORD

Joan Ganz Cooney

Originator of *Sesame Street* and

Chair, Executive Committee, Children's Television Workshop

Children and television are a potent combination, as advertisers, educators, and especially kids and their parents know. Using this enormously influential medium to benefit rather than harm or exploit children has been our aim at the Children's Television Workshop since its founding 26 years ago. This practical little book—chock-full of common sense—gives parents the tools to control and use the power of TV for their kids' education and enjoyment.

Milton Chen is one of the most knowledgeable and insightful thinkers we have in the field of children's television. I first met him more than 20 years ago, when he was a brilliant college student with an avid interest in how the media could be used to teach. While still at Harvard, he conducted research on CTW's *Electric Company.* Later he became research director for CTW's award-winning science series, *3-2-1 Contact,* and has served on a number of advisory committees for our mathematics series, *Square One TV,* and our literacy series, *Ghostwriter.* For *3-2-1 Contact,* he and the research team conducted more than 50 studies with more than 10,000 children and teachers, accumulating one of the most extensive bodies of research anywhere on what works in children's TV.

Dr. Chen has also seen the benefits of active use of video in the home and the classroom through his work with teachers, parents, and childcare providers at KQED-San Francisco. The KQED Center for Education & Lifelong Learning is a national model of how a PBS station can support its broadcasting with additional services to its community, such as workshops, teleconferences, newsletters, partnerships, and even a computer network for educators, called Learning Link.

This book combines his professional knowledge of the educational power of children's television with his own personal and practical experiences as a father and husband. He has observed, as only a parent can, the positive and negative aspects of TV in the life of his seven-year-old daughter and, especially, has seen how the best children's programs can be interwoven with books, games, activities, the classroom, the museum, and the computer to make the whole world available to a child.

It's been said that "children don't come with owner's manuals." *The Smart Parent's Guide to Kids' TV* is just that for parents who want to be responsible owners of TV sets and caregivers to their children. By setting the record straight on TV's real effects, and giving creative tips on how families can use TV for educational purposes, Dr. Chen has provided a much-needed service to parents, educators, producers, policymakers, and all of us who care about improving children's television.

This book should be packaged with every new TV and VCR sold to a parent, just as a sample of detergent comes with a washing machine. It will help you and your child take a fresh look at TV and start using it as a tool for education and enjoyment in your home.

PREFACE

Peggy Charren

Founder, Action for Children's Television

As Milton Chen's *The Smart Parent's Guide to Kids' TV* makes clear, few things in our culture can match television's extraordinary ability to touch children and influence how they think and behave. This book provides an informative, thoughtful examination of the steps parents can take to make TV viewing an enriching experience for the whole family.

I started Action for Children's Television (ACT) in 1968 to encourage more choices in children's television fare and to eliminate commercial abuses targeted to children. More than 25 years later, it seems clear that almost everyone in the commercial TV business is still trying to figure out how to benefit from children instead of how to benefit them. This approach is particularly offensive since in the US, one in four of TV's youngest viewers are poor, one in five is at risk of becoming a teen parent, and one in seven is likely to drop out of school.

Television cannot be blamed for the problems of poverty, but it can be part of the solution to improving the lives of children at risk. Television programs that speak to a child's need to know, to the need for self-esteem or for coping skills, can make a difference. Television can empower young people to get involved in efforts to improve the neighborhood, the town, the planet. Television can help children understand the rights and responsibilities of citizenship. But TV will not work to serve children without the involvement of parents, which is why this parent's guide is so important.

Milton Chen helps us understand who calls the shots in the world of television. As licensed public trustees, broadcasters have been required by law to serve the public interest. The Children's Television Act of 1990, which ACT helped to make happen, breaks new ground by specifying that service to children is a part of this obligation and that the child audience requires special consideration.

Under the new law, stations must limit the amount of advertising aired on children's TV and must broadcast some programs that meet children's educational needs. The law also established a process by which citizens can hold local stations accountable, including a legal challenge that could lead to the loss of the license to broadcast.

At the moment, commercial stations are ignoring this new educational mandate and are concentrating instead on TV's ability to amuse. Unfortunately, TV is often used to showcase violence, raunchy rock rhymes, and sexual innuendo. Many adults, frustrated and angry with this television fare and deeply concerned about TV's connection to murder and mayhem in schools and neighborhoods, want the government to ban violent TV shows and to censor language and lyrics not suitable for children.

But government censorship is not the way to protect children from television's violent content. The right to express what some consider offensive speech is the price Americans pay for freedom of political speech. And we cannot afford to risk losing that freedom.

The chief responsibility for what children see must rest with parents. This book will remind us to teach our children that violence is not the solution to problems, and that we need to use the off-button more often. It will help us to turn off what's terrible and turn on what's terrific. My favorite part of this guide is the section where Dr. Chen describes the nutritious menu of public broadcasting programs designed to excite children's minds and imaginations.

And speaking of choices, the stage is being set for a communications revolution with 500 lanes in a "telecommunications superhighway." Tomorrow's TV sets will be interactive and computer-connected, hooked up to catalogs and countries.

If knowledge is power, what do we do about the fact that the new communications technology may work against the interests of those who are poor? We cannot afford to divide the TV audience into informational haves and have-nots. Today, public broadcasting funding makes possible viewing alternatives that educate as they entertain. We must plan now to allocate support for services the commercial marketplace will not provide, to set aside a significant percentage of what Washington calls the "National Information Infrastructure" for public uses of media.

Parents and anyone else concerned with children and education need to get involved in efforts to guarantee affordable access to programs and services designed to help children and families, such as "parenting" channels on how to raise healthy and happy children; noncommercial children's channels, featuring the best in children's shows from around the world; interactive educational video games designed to attract girls as well as boys; and programs produced by young people. We need to turn TV from a Pandora's box to an Aladdin's lamp!

The Smart Parent's Guide to Kids' TV can get us started!

Introduction

FROM A CHILD OF TV TO A CAREER IN CHILDREN'S TELEVISION

Like nearly everyone in my baby-boomer generation, I am a child of television. In an old family photograph, my older sister and I sit on our parents' laps, a black-and-white TV set behind us. We are the first generation to live our entire lives under the steady glare of the TV screen. But I could not have anticipated that I would devote my career to working in educational television.

It began with a serendipitous match, more than 20 years ago. I went to the right school, for the wrong reason. As a student at Harvard College, I had intentions of becoming a lawyer, but I was intrigued by the success of a new show that broke new ground in using TV to educate young children. The show was *Sesame Street*. In the fall of 1971, I wrote a letter to Joan Ganz Cooney, president of the new production company, the Children's Television Workshop (CTW), asking whether I could get involved.

3

In the midst of *Sesame Street*'s phenomenal success and publicity, she wrote me back. She said all I needed to do was walk across campus and see Professor Gerald Lesser at the Harvard Graduate School of Education, who happened to be the chairman of CTW's board of advisers. At the time, you could have counted on one hand the number of professors in this country interested in using TV to teach.

Gerry was likewise gracious and encouraging, and, along with other students, we began a project watching children watch *The Electric Company*, CTW's newest series on reading. We observed classrooms of second- and third-graders, quizzed them about what they liked and understood, and relayed their feedback to CTW producers in New York, who were immersed in completing the first season of the program.

Watching Kids Watch—and Learn

As part of the project, we went to a school in Boston's Chinatown. Minutes before the broadcast, the students filed into the school auditorium to watch the program. (This was long before videocassettes, so programs had to be viewed at the time of broadcast.)

We wheeled a large black-and-white TV set onto the stage. Since many of the children in the audience spoke Chinese as their native language, I was uncertain how they would view this program, whose main objective was to teach English phonics and early reading skills.

The Electric Company was a fast, funny, and irreverent show. When the program's catchy theme song came on—"We're gonna turn it on, we're gonna give you the power"—a chorus of young voices instantly joined in. In segment after segment, as words appeared on the screen, the students read them aloud. They laughed at the sight gags, called out the names of their favorite characters—played by Morgan Freeman, Rita Moreno, and Bill Cosby—and danced to the songs played by the teen rock band The Short Circuits.

I was amazed and impressed. The children were practicing reading skills as they watched—and they were having fun doing it. These seven- and eight-year-olds, many children of immigrants, many from non–English speaking families, felt totally at home with the conventions of this unmistakably American series, with its zany humor, its street-smart characters, and its unusual invitation to read words off a television screen.

But then I realized that even though I had not grown up in Chinatown, I had been one of these children, too. I grew up on the south side of Chicago. I was the child of immigrants from China, who came to this country in the 1940s and decided to stay after the Communist Revolution. And I had grown up watching *The Mickey Mouse Club* and *The Ed Sullivan Show*, instantly adopting TV and its culture as my own.

My generation, growing up in the 1950s and '60s, did not have the benefit of children's programming that sought to educate and inspire us, to show us a wider world beyond our own. (That would await the vision of Joan Ganz Cooney and the premiere of *Sesame Street* in 1969.)

Instead, we had children's television that sought to entertain us; we had cartoons such as *Huckleberry Hound* and *Yogi Bear*, puppets like Kukla, Fran, and Ollie, or a local Chicago favorite,

The Frazier Thomas Show. This show featured a large canine puppet, Beauregard Burnside III, who would constantly fall asleep, at which point the program's host, Mr. Thomas, would yell in his ear, "Hot dogs, hamburgers, spaghetti, and meatballs!" To this day, these are a few of my favorite things.

Mother and Father Knew Best

Our mother and father allowed us to watch television for an hour or two in the afternoons after school. As a young boy, I enjoyed watching these shows with my older sister. I once broke my collarbone racing down a flight of stairs to watch *Huckleberry Hound.* But we also received another strong message from our parents: Television viewing was a specific activity. Programs were to be selected, each viewing session had an ending, and the TV set was not to be left on indiscriminately. We were not allowed to watch much TV in the evenings, especially programs with violence. My father was dead set against us looking at cop shows and shoot-outs, much as I was intrigued by them.

Many times I felt deprived, as my friends would chatter on about who did what to whom on last night's *I, Spy, The Man from U.N.C.L.E.,* or *The Jetsons.* But I do remember evenings spent together as a family with *The Ed Sullivan Show* or the Olympics. I would also watch the *CBS Evening News* with my father. I didn't understand much of the news, but I did get the message that it was important to be interested in events beyond our own home, city, and country. My parents did recognize my interest in sports and gave me a blue-and-white Mitsubishi transistor radio in a leather carrying case. I spent many evenings listening to ball games and the misbegotten adventures of the Chicago White Sox.

Perhaps I became enamoured of the mass media by listening to that little radio.

I am telling you something about my own upbringing because—after 20 years in children's television and seven years as a father, after conducting numerous studies with children about television and reading a lot of research done by others, and after 30 years of technological changes that bring us more viewing options—I return to some simple ideas my parents taught me, without much comment, about the role TV should play in families that care about education. In many ways, their approach to TV is an approach I offer to you.

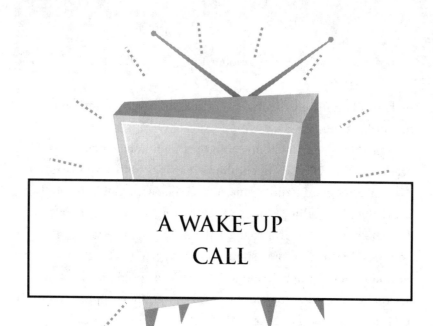

A WAKE-UP
CALL

For several years, KQED-San Francisco has conducted projects in Northern California to help children and parents use TV more wisely. We have even taken the unusual step of running on-air announcements telling children to stop sitting there and read a book or go out to play. The *New York Times* once described one of our projects by saying, "San Francisco may have the only television program that encourages viewers to turn their sets off."

I began thinking about writing this book several years ago when I observed how our daughter, Maggie, then a preschooler, enjoyed and learned from *Sesame Street* and other children's TV series and videos. I noticed how the content of many segments, whether about food from different cultures or different animals, came up in books we read and visits to street fairs or the zoo.

I also had the chance to talk with many parents in workshops and in focus groups during the KQED Parents Project, funded by the Corporation for Public Broadcasting to consider ways in which public television could better serve the needs of families.

However, I've discovered a strange thing about television and parents. We don't talk about it. It's almost a taboo topic.

As important as television is in the lives of our children, occupying more time than any other waking activity, we rarely discuss how much or what they watch, or what they get from those shows. Maybe we think it's irrelevant or unimportant. Or maybe we're embarrassed by what our kids watch or the topic itself.

This book is intended as a wake-up call to help you become more conscious of the role television plays in your child's life and in your own. I have found that once parents start talking about their kids' TV, we have a lot to say and learn from each other. The hard part is getting started.

This book is not a series of prescriptions, a system of rules that parents and children can follow to reach the Promised TV Land. This book *is* intended to offer guidance and information to help you, as a parent, become a more informed consumer of children's television. I join with other educational and media organizations in recommending that viewing be kept to an average of less than two hours a day. But I have been impressed by the different ways families arrive at that measure of control.

This book is about changing your family's relationship to television. How you choose to do so will reflect your family's background, interests, and commitment. In Parts I and II of this book, I give my views on what parenting is all about and some background on television commercial content and messages. Parts III and IV discuss how you can take control of your family viewing through a Family TV Diet and connect educational shows with other learning experiences.

Part V looks at other media, such as computers and video games, and at how to apply the book's general ideas to current and future electronic media that we use in the home.

In this book, you'll read many examples of educational children's programs on public television, as well as examples of quality children's programs on commercial channels and on videos. However, because public TV has the best concentration of educational programs but the smallest budgets to promote them, I do emphasize those programs I know best. As we discovered in our focus groups for the Parents Project, many parents are unaware of the range of quality educational children's programs available.

Because I'm a busy parent, too, I've probably started more books than I've finished. Therefore, I have purposefully organized this book into short chapters so that you can pick it up and read it in many short sittings, almost like a magazine. It's a "random-access book:" You can start anywhere and finish anywhere, and you need not pick up where you left off.

A word about usage: I use "parent" to include moms or dads, single, step, foster, gay, or grand; and "parenting" to mean either singly or together. Just as there are many different configurations for families, there are many different parental relationships.

To sum it up in one phrase, the main point of this book is this: Children's television should become parents' television. By becoming more aware, more conscious, and more knowledgeable about the television our children watch, we'll become better parents. More importantly, our children will be better prepared for the future. It's time to bring the topic of TV out of the closet.

PART I

You Are Your Child's Most Important Teacher

TV: FROM THE BOOB TUBE TO A TEST TUBE FOR LEARNING

If you are reading this book, you already have some concerns about the role of television in your child's life. Television—it's been called The Boob Tube. The Plug-In Drug. The One-Eyed Monster. The Lowest Common Denominator.

That's the bad news. The good news is the boob tube can also be a test tube for learning in your home. But to make it so requires you to take a closer look at what the medium does well and what it does poorly. Turning that knowledge into action takes a commitment from you and your child. And, as with any effective parenting, it takes experimenting with this test tube to see what works for your own family.

Fortunately, if you've decided to read this book, you are already committed to the most important job on the planet— being an educator for your child. Parents *are* teachers. When it comes to the education of our children, we should put to rest all the fine distinctions between teachers, educators, parents, guardians, and caregivers.

Every adult with whom a child spends significant time is an educator for that child. They are responsible for how the child is spending her most precious resource—her time.

Kids Are Learning Every Moment

Today, some educators still insist that since parents are not "trained" as educators, they should refrain from actually attempting to teach their children skills such as reading, mathematics, or science. This is hogwash.

I prefer the enlightened view of one California grade-school teacher who was asked what message she would most like to convey to parents. She responded, "Tell them that they are teaching their kids every moment, every day, and they do more good or harm than we as teachers ever can."

She told me about a parents' conference at which a third-grader's parent asked, "I see the homework coming home, and my daughter seems to be doing fine. But I have one question: When is she *really* going to start learning?"

This mother had in mind "The Great Leap Forward" model of her daughter's development. She was expecting too much from the school and ignoring the educational foundation that should have been laid by her, childcare providers, and others in the seven years leading up to that conference. This foundation—her daughter's interest in learning as well as her image of herself as "a learner"—was, for the most part, already set. Most of her time in school would be devoted to gradually filling in a knowledge base in different subject areas.

In It for the Long Haul

Much like one's health, what we do every day, every week, and every year makes a difference in the state of our children's education. Educating a child is not a matter of dormant periods, followed by explosive "learning growth spurts." If you're a parent, and you're interested in having a thoughtful, imaginative, curious, and well-educated child, you're in it for the long haul.

You're also more important in this process than traditional thinking on education has been willing to admit. Education reform efforts have begun to address how parents can work in concert with schools and community organizations to focus on "the whole child." And once we focus on the home, we must also focus on how time is spent in the home—which is why television is also a major educator.

EVERY CHILD IS GIFTED AND TALENTED

As parents, we rarely discuss our goals for our children or, for that matter, for ourselves. What kind of kids are we trying to raise? What are we trying to accomplish as their parents?

Take a moment and think about this. What are three or four goals for your children (e.g., to be honest and responsible, to find happiness, to be financially secure)? What are some goals for yourself as their parent (e.g., to give them a safe home and to help them feel secure, to provide for their physical and emotional needs)?

Like most parents, my wife, Ruth, and I are concerned that our daughter, Maggie, grow up with the right values, such as having a strong inner compass about right versus wrong and treating others with respect and compassion. But we also have educational goals for our daughter, which is why we take seriously the quality of education in her preschool and her public school. Our educational goal is simply this: to help her discover her talents. I believe that every child is talented, even multitalented. I also believe that every child is wired to learn.

Television can be a parent's partner in helping a child to discover his talents. Educational TV shows can become part of a "learning environment" established by parents in the home. A *Nature* watcher might start a bug collection, and a *Reading Rainbow* fan might write his family's history. The key factor is parents who recognize the major role they have to play.

However, many children do not receive the attention and affection they deserve and need help to develop their gifts. Even in Maggie's classroom, some six- and seven-year-olds already believe they cannot read, draw, or perform in a play. They seem starved for attention and affection, a word of encouragement, a pat on the back. If an important goal for parents and educators is to help our children find and develop their talents, the use of TV becomes a central issue, because it can both support as well as undermine our efforts.

The Problem with Labels

Now, talent is a funny word. We say someone is "talented" when we feel they have some special, God-given gift. We've even enshrined the word in our educational jargon—GATE programs in our schools stand for Gifted and Talented Education. Only a small number of kids—the less than 10 percent who pass a battery of tests—is allowed into GATE programs. Since most of our kids are not in GATE programs, we assume they must not be gifted and talented.

Attaching labels to children—"the gifted," "remedial readers," "problem students"—is one of the most destructive aspects of our social and educational systems. Labels allow the educational system to discriminate and provide a better quality of education to those with the "good labels." They also excuse us from having higher goals for the rest of our children. And they create expectations—in parents, teachers, and most of all, children themselves.

As many good teachers and coaches know, students rise to the level of our expectations. If we believe our children can learn, we will behave toward them in ways that will support their

Sticks and Stones and Names *Can* Hurt Me

Since the 1960s, researchers have been looking at how children are affected by teacher and parent expectations. In one 1968 study, Harvard psychologist Robert Rosenthal and his colleague Lenore Jacobson told elementary-school teachers that a test had been developed to identify students who were poised to make rapid academic advancements. They then told the teachers which students in the classes were going to be the "bloomers."

At the end of the school year, the bloomers had indeed outperformed the other students. There was just one problem. These students had been selected randomly. Rosenthal and Jacobson believed that the teachers encouraged and supported the bloomers more than the other students, due to their expectations that these students were capable of making great strides. Since that study, many others have also shown that teachers treat students differently based on their beliefs about the students' abilities.

learning. We will spend time with them, encourage them, make the extra effort to surround them with positive experiences. And they will respond and believe they can learn—and will enjoy learning. They'll even get the most powerfully motivating idea of all—that they're good at it.

My Son, the Genius?

One of the best known educational researchers in the world, Dr. Benjamin Bloom, and his colleagues at the University of Chicago conducted another revealing study about the power of labels, encouragement, and talent.

As they report in their book *Developing Talent in Young People*, Bloom and his colleagues studied 120 high-achieving men and women, the best in the world in six fields. These young individuals, most under 35, included concert pianists, sculptors, mathematicians, scientists, and tennis champions.

These are the sorts of people we view as "geniuses," born with unusual gifts that predestine them to greatness. Surely, someone must have identified their innate talents at an early age. These young prodigies must have been separated from their parents and rushed off to the nearest university physics department or to Pancho Segura's tennis camp for special tutelage.

Quite to the contrary, Bloom found that these talented individuals grew up in homes where there was no revelation of "genius" at an early age, no single-minded focus on a specific skill or activity, and no pushy parents in the wings.

He found that their early years were characterized by a nurturing family environment, in which parents emphasized intellectual curiosity, hard work, and responsibility. As children, these individuals exhibited a range of interests and were not narrowly focused. Their parents encouraged them to explore a variety of activities, with an emphasis on enjoyment of learning. Then, Bloom explains, this form of "play and recreation" was "followed by a long sequence of learning activities that involve high standards, much time, and a great deal of hard work."

Bloom found that these parents awakened their children's curiosity, encouraged them to ask questions, and engaged them in a process of finding answers:

> The parents valued academic achievement and were models of intellectual behavior. Perhaps the most significant aspect of these early years was the way the parents responded to their children's questions. Questions were treated seriously, and when the parents didn't know the answers, they taught their children how and where to find them. These parents believed that their children were special and shared with them the excitement of discovery.... Learning how to learn was more important than what they learned.

"What any person in the world can learn, almost all persons can learn," writes Bloom. He believes that nearly every child is capable of such achievements. Whether it's science or the saxophone, talent is not something in our genes, dispensed at conception, but a matter of parental encouragement, a child's curiosity, and many hours spent in activities cultivating a child's talents.

So parents, heed Dr. Bloom's words. When you look at your child, think of her as special, talented, capable of great things. In Garrison Keillor's whimsical *Lake Wobegon*, "All the children are above average." I believe they got that way because their parents, determined Midwesterners, refused to believe their kids are only average.

If you remember these two studies, you'll set the right frame for everything that is to follow in this book. Because, contrary to much public opinion, television can actually help your child develop his gifts.

RACING THE CLOCK: YOU HAVE LESS TIME THAN YOU THINK

Parents play the major role in helping a child understand the world and love learning. But you don't have 18 years to do it; the patterns are set by about age eight. By then, most of a young person's personality traits and attitudes about learning are in place. Many child development experts say that even infants and toddlers are learning more than we think. They're just waiting until they have the language skills to let us know.

Parents and other adults don't have much time to help set these patterns. A superintendent of an urban school district once told me that he can walk into a fourth-grade classroom and tell who won't be in school five years later. Students who look sad or bored, who are angry or fight often, or who look undernourished or abused are already showing signs that predict they will be school dropouts.

First You're Changing Her Diapers—Then She's Driving

When you're the parent of a newborn child, it's hard to look down the long road ahead. When my daughter was born, Ruth and I saw in her all the promise of a long, loving, and productive life ahead. But we scarcely could contemplate what she might be like today, seven years later. We focused on feeding her, changing her diapers, and getting some sleep.

Gradually, though, our time horizons for Maggie have lengthened. Although she is only seven, I can imagine what her life will be like five and even 10 years from now. And Ruth and I can map out some steps we need to take in order to support her continued development. While our job is far from done, I do have the distinct sense that halftime is over.

> One in four Americans say they are so attached to television that they wouldn't surrender their TV sets for $1 million.
> —TV Guide *poll, June 1992*

TV: The Thief of Time

How does this relate to television? Because television is the default activity in most homes, it can easily consume too many hours of your child's life. The amount of time American children spend watching TV is staggering: an average of four hours a day, 28 hours a week, 1,400 hours a year, close to 18,000 hours by the time a child graduates from high school. Compare that with the 13,000 hours children spend in school, from kindergarten

A Family's Effective Use of Television

Several years ago, I received this inspiring letter from a mother, who, without many financial resources, is actively using educational TV broadcasts to further her children's learning at home.

Dear Mr. Milton Chen,

My children and I have been enjoying KQED's children's programming for nine years now. I really restrict TV watching at my house. What they do watch must be quality TV, usually educational. That is why we enjoy Channel 9 so much.

We especially utilize your summer programming. We watch nature programs, then take trips to the library to find books on the subject you introduced to us. We discuss environmental issues and learn about many species of birds, mammals, reptiles, fish, and plant life. We travel to far off countries through your programs about different cultures. We are half Pueblo Native American, so all your Indian programming is of great interest to us. My children excel in science and social studies at school, which I definitely attribute to your shows.

Our main reason we use your...programming is because we are low-income apartment dwellers. There is no money for vacations, and I don't allow my children to just hang out doing nothing all day. Time is not redeemable.

They are reading and writing and improving their skills and enjoying every minute of it....I can get some housework done in the morning knowing they are *not* seeing sex, drugs, violence, or unacceptable, mindless trashy TV. You help fill our summer in a positive way. Many of our friends agree. Thanks for all you do and keep up the good work.

—Cordially yours,
Mrs. Rhonda E. Garcia

through twelfth grade. *Kids spend more time watching TV than any other activity,* save sleeping.

Time spent in front of the TV is time a child isn't playing, reading, drawing, or helping out with a chore. Dr. Reginald Clark, a lecturer and consultant at California State University at Fullerton, has spent more than a decade studying high achievers at the elementary and high school levels. He finds that these students come from "effective families" who share not levels of income, education, or race, but traits, such as feeling in control of their lives, holding high expectations of children, a view of hard work as a key to success, and an active lifestyle.

Clark has also found that these children, including many from lower-income backgrounds, spend a substantial amount of time engaged in learning and enrichment activities in the home. The key to these activities lies in the families' perspective: They recognized the wide variety of activities that offer learning opportunities and valued them. On average, these children spent 25 to 35 hours in what Clark calls "home-centered learning," such as homework, reading, hobbies, games, sports, household chores, family outings, community youth programs, and part-time jobs.

But You Don't Have to Toss Out the TV

Obviously, in one week a child cannot watch 30 hours of television, pursue 30 hours of learning activities, go to school or daycare, eat, and sleep. Something has got to give.

To simply throw out the TV and replace the hours your child spends watching it with wonderful and stimulating activities would be a daunting task for most parents. In our own lives, something's got to give.

The good news is you don't have to throw out the television. TV, in moderation, can play a positive role in your child's learning. In Part IV, "Weaving a Web of Learning for Your Child," I'll discuss ways in which TV viewing and related activities can become part of your child's "home-centered learning."

PART II

The Stranger in the House: What TV Teaches Our Kids

THE MEDIUM IS NOT THE MESSAGE: "IT'S THE CONTENT, STUPID!"

The most important point of this book is quite simple. During the 1992 presidential campaign, Clinton campaign director James Carville posted a sign in his office to remind him to stick to his most powerful theme: "It's the economy, stupid!" In considering the effect of television on kids, we must also keep reminding ourselves: "It's the content, stupid!"

> "Parents have to realize that there is a stranger in your house. If you came home and you found a strange man…teaching your kids to punch each other, or trying to sell them all kinds of products, you'd kick him right out of the house. But here you are; you come in and the TV is on; and you don't think twice about it."
> —Dr. Jerome Singer, professor of psychology, Yale University, as quoted in the TV series On Television

The real issue is not the electronic box, but what's on it. This book rests on two pillars: control and content. We need to *control* the amount and types of television our children watch and use the *content* of educational programs as a springboard for further learning activities.

TV, the Media Whipping Boy

As parents, we are understandably concerned about how TV affects our children. And, as with most complex and controversial topics, supposed experts disagree on its effects.

Unfortunately, a number of television "experts" have promoted some fuzzy but provocative ideas about television's effects, in books, magazine articles, and on the talk-show circuit. Many of their ideas trace their lineage to that well-known media guru, Marshall McLuhan, and his famous adage from the 1960s: "The medium is the message." McLuhan provided some thought-provoking analyses of television, radio, and books and the ways in which they communicate information to their audiences.

But McLuhan was a philosopher. He didn't conduct any studies of TV viewers. He wasn't trying to tell us whether TV was good or bad, or how it affects kids.

Since McLuhan, some academics and writers have taken up the battle cry that television as a medium is a destructive force in the lives of our children. Marie Winn's books about TV and children, *The Plug-In Drug* and *Unplugging the Plug-In Drug,* espouse the view that television, like drugs or alcohol, is addictive. Neil Postman, a professor at New York University, believes that we are using TV for purposes of, as he titled his book, *Amusing Ourselves to*

Death. Psychologist Jane Healy, in *Endangered Minds*, says television is destroying our children's brains.

These critics use a broad brush to paint an overly sinister portrait of television. They say the solution is to turn off the tube and banish it from our lives forever. There is a kernel of truth in what they are saying. The vast majority of American television is hardly a source of national pride. But in making sweeping and alarming generalizations, their critiques have created more hysteria than informed debate.

> A 1992 *Newsweek* poll found that 49 percent of those surveyed think television is the biggest influence on children. Only 26 percent of the respondents think that parents are. And 49 percent said they think television entertainment negatively affects kids.

The Medium Is Only the Medium

With all due credit to McLuhan, the medium is only the medium. Television, like newspapers, radio, or computers, communicates a broad range of content for a wide variety of purposes. Television's tool kit—documentaries, dramas, performances, talk shows, game shows, and animations—can inform and educate as well as titillate and sell.

The key point seems obvious but is often lost in debates about TV: Content is what matters. *Sesame Street* is not *The Mighty Morphin Power Rangers*. *Roots* is not *Roseanne*. *The MacNeil-Lehrer NewsHour* is not tabloid TV. The reasons we tune in to these programs, and what we take away from them, are entirely different—even diametrically opposed.

We see the same differences in content in all media. The *New York Times* is not the *National Enquirer*. "National Public Radio" is not "The Howard Stern Show." Using computer networks, one of the newest media, students are sharing acid rain measurements with scientists, while some men are sharing child pornography. The technology is neutral. Content is critical.

Why, then, does television get fingered so often in the search for the Cultural Bad Guy? Well, TV is an easy target. It does account for an inordinate amount of time in the lives of Americans. A lot of TV programming *is* mindless, depressing, violent, insulting, and laced with relentless commercials. We *should* be critical of this medium and the ways in which Americans use it. Much of its *content* is worth criticizing. However, I do find it curious that no one is calling for the wholesale abolition of newspapers, magazines, radio, or computers.

> 98 percent of American households have TV sets. 69 percent have two or more TV sets. 33 percent have three or more sets. Per household, TV usage averages about seven hours each day.

A Smart User's Guide to Media

When it comes to these other media, we are smarter. We understand their value because we use them for certain purposes. We connect the content we're using to the media we're choosing.

But somehow, with television, we subtract 15 points from our Media IQ, and babble about how horrible television is and how it ought to be banished to media Siberia. Why the difference?

I believe it has to do with the fact that newspapers, radio, and computers, for the most part, belong to adults. But TV is a child's medium. TV has a hold on kids that other media do not. Part of our collective hysteria about television may be based on a sincere desire to protect our children. But if we really care about our children, our response should be to get smarter, not dumber, about television, to look more closely at its contents, its positives and negatives, and to use what we know to make it better.

Because TV is such an easy target, it's an easy scapegoat for all that is wrong with society. Television has single-handedly been blamed for increasing crime, reducing levels of education, destroying our values, ruining our work force, and making us fat.

Is TV the root or the fruit of so many of society's ills? If we all put our TV sets away for a year, I doubt we'd see much improvement in those problems. The real roots of our social problems are much more deeply entrenched.

But one thing is clear: Improving our society depends on improving our family life. That means equipping parents with the knowledge and skills to raise kids who are eager to learn and contribute their talents to society. It is my belief that TV, while part of the problem, can also be part of the solution.

> "This instrument can teach, it can illuminate; yes, and it can even inspire. But it can do so only to the extent that humans are determined to use it to those ends. Otherwise it is merely lights and wires in a box."
> —*Edward R. Murrow, 1958*

SIX MYTHS ABOUT TELEVISION AND CHILDREN

A curious mythology has grown up around television and its effects on children. Together, these myths would have us believe that TV is single-handedly turning kids into couch potatoes, frying their brains, shortening their attention spans, and lowering their academic abilities. Supposedly, TV is a dark and foreboding menace in our children's lives. As discussed in the previous chapter, these myths can be traced to the simplistic, yet persistent, view that TV, as a medium, has effects of its own that transcend any specific content.

Since teachers, parents, and the media themselves are constantly propagating these myths, it is important to examine them. Although some children who watch TV 30 or 40 hours a week struggle in school, there are deeper reasons why they do besides time spent watching TV. Are their parents taking an active role in helping their children learn? Or are these latchkey children who are left to their own devices? Television's effects do depend on how much we watch and, more importantly, on *what* we watch. None of the following myths are supported by substantive research. In fact, research has often contradicted them. Unfortunately, the propagators of these myths have done a much better job of marketing their opinions to the public than the researchers who have done the studies to debunk them. So here I present, in point-counterpoint fashion, six pervasive myths about TV.

MYTH #1: TV is a passive medium. My child will become a listless couch potato.

FACT #1: Educational TV shows can actively engage your child, physically and intellectually. The activity can and should continue after the show is over.

There are at least two types of passivity: physical and intellectual. One of the most common myths about TV viewing is that it is, by definition, a passive activity. Contrary to popular belief, neither physical nor intellectual passivity is an immutable fact of TV viewing, especially for children.

As any parent of a child who watches *Barney & Friends* or *Sesame Street* knows, young viewers are physically engaged, singing, clapping, and stretching along with their favorite characters, especially when the shows invite them to do so. Programs such as these also encourage intellectual activity as children learn important concepts, from counting to kindness.

One overlooked and underused feature of television is its ability to prompt viewers to read aloud. Some current children's shows, such as *Ghostwriter* and *Beakman's World*, use animation and graphics to highlight key words for viewers to read and pronounce as they are watching.

Many other examples of children's TV shows demonstrate how young viewers can exercise their cognitive muscles while they watch. A US Department of Education study found that "contrary to popular assertions, children are cognitively active during television viewing in an attempt to form a coherent, connected understanding of television programs."

The activity shouldn't cease after the show is over. The best children's programs provide activities and tips for teachers, childcare providers, and parents on related follow-up activities. Whether it's folding origami with Shari Lewis of *Lamb Chop's Play-Along*, writing a letter to *Ghostwriter*, or borrowing a *Reading Rainbow* book from the library, TV can be a creative source of active learning, rather than the presumed death of it.

> "Television may be the only electrical appliance that's more useful after it's turned off."
> —Fred Rogers, host of *Mister Rogers' Neighborhood*

MYTH #2: TV stunts the healthy growth of the brain. It zaps a child's brainwaves.

FACT #2: Brainwave patterns during TV viewing are very similar to brain activity during other activities.

Some educators and commentators, like educational psychologist Dr. Jane Healy, have suggested that TV viewing has a deleterious effect on brain development, that because it is a visual medium, it may overstimulate the right hemisphere (responsible

Making Every Program an "I Can Read" Show

Studies show that closed-captioning subtitles, originally intended to help the hearing-impaired, can encourage the reading skills of beginning readers, young and old alike. Previously, these captions were only viewable via a decoder attached to the TV set. Today, these decoders are built into American-made TV sets. Now those who need to brush up on basic reading skills, including those learning English as a second language, can practice by reading the captions, and obtain immediate reinforcement by hearing the dialogue and seeing the action. Children's "sing-along" videos, which display the lyrics on screen, also support reading skills.

for visual processing) and understimulate the left hemisphere (responsible for language and processing of print). The critique often invokes technical language about "frontal lobe development," "neural pathways," and "alpha and beta waves," creating both confusion and concern in the minds of many parents.

Does TV really interfere with children's brain functioning and zap their synapses? It can seem plausible, especially when such claims are made in jargon with the appearance of medical authority.

A neuropsychologist's authoritative review should put these fears to rest. Dr. Katharine Fite of the Neuroscience and Behavior Program at the University of Massachusetts, Amherst, recently concluded:

> In recent years, a number of claims have appeared in the popular media and press suggesting that television viewing has potentially detrimental effects on human brain development and/or brain activity. An extensive review of the published scientific literature provides no evidence to substantiate such beliefs.

Fite described two major findings from experiments that measured small electrical signals from the scalp, indicating brain activity. These studies found that during TV watching, viewers' brainwave patterns are "quite similar to those that occur during other waking state activities. Thus TV viewing should not be characterized as producing a passive or inattentive activity in the brain." She also reported that TV is not, as argued, exclusively a right-brain activity.

Parents should rest easier, knowing this alarm about our children's gray matter is only a red herring. Instead, we should devote our own brainwaves to the more important questions of what and how much our children are watching.

MYTH #3: TV shortens a child's attention span.

FACT #3: Educational TV shows can actually increase a child's attention and cognitive skills.

Myth #3 and its close cousin, Myth #2, have been propagated by a small but prolific group of writers and educators who often turn their attack on one specific program. The object of their reproach? Not *Teenage Mutant Ninja Turtles* or *The Mighty Morphin Power Rangers*. No, none other than *Sesame Street*. The critique is an academic hit-and-run, since these individuals do not stop to conduct any research of their own, nor do they cite the wealth of research that has already been done on the program.

Sesame Street is the most widely researched television program in history. In fact, a bibliography published by Children's Television Workshop (CTW) in 1989 lists an astonishing 633 studies on its cognitive and social effects.

Yet, some academics and writers insist that *Sesame Street* is a hazard to children's development. As Dr. Daniel Anderson, professor of psychology at the University of Massachusetts, Amherst, explains, these critics believe that the "rapid transitions between scenes...mesmerize children and interfere with their reflection and inference, so that the child is left only with memories of a jumbled, disconnected set of visual images."

But Anderson, who has studied the effect of *Sesame Street* on children's attention spans more thoroughly than anyone else, believes that these critics do not give young children enough credit for their purposeful cognitive skills. He summarizes the findings:

> The new research showed that the critique was wrong. The child viewer of *Sesame Street*, rather than being a mesmerized zombie, is selective and intellectually active....We have evidence that *Sesame Street* actually enhances attentional and perceptual abilities....Research on *Sesame Street* has shown us that young children are far more capable than we previously believed.

Then why is *Sesame Street* so often the target of misguided and uninformed broadsides? Dr. Samuel Ball, who conducted the first evaluations of *Sesame Street*, believes that the series was bound to be victimized by some because of its success. In Australia, he observes, "we have what we call the 'tall poppy' syndrome. When you see a tall poppy, you saw off its head, quick smart....The USA is not barren of this kind of reaction to success, either."

There are precious few genuine educational innovations in our country, and *Sesame Street* is one of them. The series' research record clearly supports its effectiveness: *Sesame Street* boasts votes of approval from the 16 million children who watch the show each week, as well as their parents, who witness their children learning from the Muppets, the music, the animation, and the characters treating each other with respect and good humor. Personally, I'd take a hundred eager kids watching *Sesame Street* over a few disgruntled academics any day.

MYTH #4: If my child watches TV, she'll be a poor student.

FACT #4: It depends on what and how much she's watching. Students who watch a moderate amount of television, especially educational TV, can be excellent students.

The research on this topic will surprise many. Dr. Keith Mielke, vice president for research at Children's Television Workshop, has examined reviews of research on the relationship of TV viewing to academic achievement.

The studies point out what is commonly touted: Very high levels of TV viewing (35 or more hours per week) negatively correlate with academic achievement. This makes sense, as children who are watching excessive amounts of TV do not have time to do much else. But several studies found that academic achievement was positively related to a moderate amount of TV viewing, on the order of 10 to 15 hours per week.

The real issue, Mielke says, is not the sheer number of hours a child watches but what programs she's watching—and how parents and teachers use programs to help maximize learning.

Probably, children who watch 40 hours of TV or more each week are not watching much educational fare. It is also likely that kids who watch a moderate amount receive some strong parental

The Difference *Sesame Street* Makes

After the first year of *Sesame Street*, an extensive evaluation was conducted to see if the program made a difference in preschoolers' cognitive and emotional skills. Two psychologists from the Educational Testing Service, Dr. Samuel Ball and Dr. Sandra Bogatz, inaugurated the first of hundreds of studies on the program. In one of their studies, they found that children from all backgrounds who watched *Sesame Street* regularly for six months learned more numbers, letters, and other cognitive skills than those who did not watch. The regular viewers also learned more about their emotions than the nonviewers.

Twenty years later, kids are still learning: A 1990 study shows that three- to five-year-olds who watch the program have improved vocabularies.

messages about what to watch as well as what to do with the rest of their time, with an educational focus.

MYTH #5: If my child watches TV, he won't become a good reader. TV and books are enemies.

FACT #5: Quality children's programs can actually motivate children to read books and lead to a love of reading.

This curious and widespread belief holds that TV viewing is antithetical to book reading and that kids who watch TV will not be good readers. I believe this myth is tied to a larger cultural bias: an intellectual snobbery, in favor of books and against TV.

Joan Ganz Cooney, originator of *Sesame Street* and founder of the Children's Television Workshop (CTW), clarifies the issue: "Thoughtful people would not argue that because children read comic books, they should not therefore do any additional reading in school. Yet they apply a similar argument to the medium of television."

This pro-book, anti-TV bias doesn't stand up against the evidence of specific TV shows, such as *Reading Rainbow*, that encourage the reading of books. After viewing this program, children are so excited to get their hands on *Reading Rainbow* that librarians and bookstore owners report dramatically increased circulations and sales. In one study, 86 percent of children's librarians said the series was responsible for increased circulation. Mimi Kayden, director of children's marketing for E. P. Dutton, has said, "Books that would sell 5,000 copies on their own sell 25,000 copies if they're on *Reading Rainbow*."

This phenomenon occurs with just about every other popular children's TV show with book and magazine tie-ins. Publishers understand this synergy between TV broadcasts and book sales very well, which explains the many children's books based upon popular characters on children's TV.

A series of *Ghostwriter* books, published just a year ago, has already sold thousands of copies. *Sesame Street* children's books have been best-sellers for more than two decades. *Sesame Street Magazine* is a leading magazine among families with preschoolers, and is accompanied by the excellent *Sesame Street Parent's Guide*. Book classics such as *Anne of Green Gables* enjoy renewed sales when their stories are televised.

This phenomenon is certainly not limited to children. Ken Burns' *The Civil War*, Bill Moyers' *Healing and the Mind*, and

James Burke's *Connections*, each based on a PBS series, have been best-selling books. After watching a particularly innovative or moving TV show, viewers want to read a book related to it.

MYTH #6: If my child watches TV shows that entertain as well as educate, he'll expect his teachers to sing and dance.

FACT #6: Even young children understand the separate worlds and conventions of TV and the classroom.

One of the strangest myths about children's television is that children who watch Barney and Big Bird will set unrealistic expectations about their teachers' dramatic talents. There is no research to support this notion, nor do teachers report pupils urging them to break out in song or do a little soft-shoe while at the blackboard. Even preschoolers understand what behaviors are appropriate for which situations. I know of no reports in which a child has pointed a make-believe remote at a teacher and attempted to click him off.

Do quality children's programs delude children and their parents into confusing "entertainment" with "education"? Media pundit Neil Postman, in his book, *Amusing Ourselves to Death*, contends that this is exactly the problem with educational shows such as *Sesame Street* or *The Voyage of the Mimi*, an award-winning series on science and mathematics.

Education, as Postman defines it, is what goes on in the traditional classroom—teacher at the head of the class, students dutifully listening—and entertainment is what television does, using celebrities, music, animation, and other cheap thrills. To him, the two are like oil and water.

Education is much more than mere "schooling," but too often we have squeezed the passion and excitement from learning in the classroom. We have disconnected many subjects, such as history, science, and art, from the true sense of joy and curiosity that animates the historians, scientists, and artists who have made professions out of them. Sadly, we have made learning dull.

> "Students [can] learn...present-day subject matter in a third or less of the present time, pleasurably rather than painfully....Education in a new and greatly broadened sense can become a lifelong pursuit for everyone. To go on learning...[is] a purpose worthy of humankind's ever-expanding capacities. Education, at best, is ecstatic."
> —George Leonard, *Education and Ecstasy*

Learning Is a Volunteer Activity

Our job as parents and teachers should be to make learning joyful, stimulating, and, as George Leonard says, ecstatic. In our culture, there is a strong belief that learning is serious, hard work.

But the way to get young children interested in embarking on this process is to expose them to the joys of learning early on. If television can help in this regard, so much the better. When we label *Sesame Street* or *NOVA* as sheer "entertainment," we ignore the ways in which TV programs can use video technology and appealing characters to reveal the compelling nature of a subject.

Instead of condemning TV for communicating this revolutionary idea, we should focus on making other educational experiences more lively and engaging. The best children's museums and science centers do this. They are places where kids want to go, where they are learning while they are actively engaged with exhibits, museum staff, teachers, parents, and each other.

In the end, learning is a voluntary activity. Whether we're six or 60, we can't be forced to learn. TV viewing in the home is also a voluntary activity, something your children do because they want to, for positive as well as not-so-positive reasons. The fact that children like TV is something we can build on. When TV is well designed, it can appeal not only to their funny bones but to their hearts and minds as well.

RISING VIOLENCE IN OUR STREETS AND ON OUR SCREENS

In the San Francisco Bay Area, 15-year-old Cecelia Rios, a model student and former president of her student council, was stabbed to death in a high-school stairwell by another teenager. In New York, Jacob Gonzales, 10, and Damien Dorris, 14, murdered Elizabeth Alvarez, a pregnant mother of three, near an automated teller machine.

The FBI reports in 1993 that there were 1.9 million violent crimes in the US, including 24,500 murders, 104,600 rapes, 659,000 robberies, and 1.1 million assaults. Compared to levels of interpersonal violence in other countries, the US leads the world. Our homicide rate, at 8 per 100,000, is more than double the next

The average American child will have watched 100,000 acts of televised violence, including 8,000 murders, by the time he or she finishes sixth grade.

highest rate, in Finland, and four to eight times higher than rates in Israel, Canada, Sweden, Scotland, and Australia, for example.

Violence has become an American way of life. We are the most violent society on the face of the earth—and our fastest rising crime category is violence committed by youth.

The Most Violent TV in the World

Americans can also claim the dubious award of having the most violent television in the world, for years running. Over the past two decades, the level of TV violence has been remarkably steady, report researchers Dr. George Gerbner, dean emeritus of the University of Pennsylvania's Annenberg School of Communications, and Dr. Nancy Signorielli of the University of Delaware, who have studied patterns of violent content on American TV. An average evening's prime-time programming contains about 16 violent acts, including two murders.

Once Upon a Time in a Place with No TV

Some of the most compelling studies have investigated children's behavior in areas before and after the introduction of television. In the early 1970s, Dr. Tannis Macbeth Williams and other researchers from the University of British Columbia compared the levels of aggression in first- and second-graders from two Canadian towns— one with access to TV and one, due to a mountain range, with no TV access. When the mountain town finally received television, the hitting, biting, and shoving levels of the children increased by 160 percent.

The Mean World Syndrome

How do thousands of hours spent watching TV violence affect viewers? Dr. George Gerbner, dean emeritus of the University of Pennsylvania's Annenberg School of Communications, believes that one of the real dangers of pervasive TV violence is viewers' increasing perception that the world is, indeed, a mean and dangerous place.

In their 1994 TV Violence Profile, Gerbner and his colleagues Drs. Michael Morgan and Nancy Signorielli explain that long-term, regular exposure to television can contribute to people's sense of vulnerability, dependence, and desensitization to violence. They also found that heavy viewers are more likely than light viewers to believe that their neighborhood is unsafe, that crime is a very serious personal problem, and that they are likely to be involved in violence. These heavy viewers are also more likely to buy new locks, watchdogs, and even guns for protection. The researchers say that their belief in a "mean world" full of danger and menace "invites not only aggression but also exploitation and repression. That is the deeper problem of violence-laden television."

"Crime in prime time is at least 10 times as rampant as in the real world, and an average of five to six acts of overt physical violence per hour involve well over half of all major characters."
—*Michael Morgan, University of Massachusetts, Amherst*

Dial TV for Murder, 24 Hours a Day

One of the cardinal rules of TV economics is that it is much cheaper to buy an old program than to create a new one. In the scramble to fill air time, TV stations often turn to series reruns, which cost far less than a new program. And many of those series are highly violent. If you flip through the cable channels on a typical night, you'll see many reruns of violent shows from years gone by.

The result is that, as Newton Minow points out on page 52, the addition of more channels makes it *easier* for a child to view violence. And if cheap reruns weren't bad enough, we also have to contend with the new genre of "reality TV," shows such as *Cops* or *Rescue 911*, featuring live footage and reenactments of violent crimes. There is a 24-hour barrage of shootings, assaults, murders, and break-ins somewhere on your TV dial—and a child can watch it all.

Kids themselves feel that violence on TV has gone too far. The 1993 Yankelovich Youth Monitor interviewed a national random sampling of 1,200 children between the ages of six and 17. Among the nine- to 17-year-olds who were asked, *more than two-thirds of the children thought there was too much violence on TV*. Even higher percentages of girls and inner-city kids agreed with this statement.

> In the average hour of children's TV programming, there are 26 violent acts; during an average prime-time hour, there are 5.

Unconscionable Numbers

Imagine a child watching 8,000 murders by the time she's 12! How does the constant avalanche of TV's violent images affect children? What is the relationship between the viewing of TV violence and children's aggressive behavior?

These questions have been the subject of more research studies than any other in the history of social science. In the last 30 years, researchers have conducted more than 1,000 studies on some aspect of TV violence. There have been surveys of children, their parents, and their teachers; experiments conducted in university labs; and longitudinal studies in which researchers have followed young people, their TV viewing, and their behaviors over a number of years.

The subject is complex and controversial. But the weight of the research supports the link between the viewing of TV violence and aggressive behavior. When other positive influences, such as parents and teachers, are not actively present in a young person's life, the linkage is even stronger. The only consistent research minimizing the effects of TV violence has been sponsored by the commercial networks.

A 1993 *Los Angeles Times* poll found that 4 out of 5 Americans think television violence contributes to real life violence. More than half of those surveyed would support government guidelines to limit TV violence. In 1993, 80 percent of adults surveyed by Times-Mirror felt that TV violence was harmful to society; in 1983, only 64 percent thought so.

TV Violence and Tobacco:
Harmful to Your Child's Health

The situation is similar to the battle between the US Surgeon General and the tobacco industry. Although the research conducted by tobacco interests tells a different story, the position of the US Surgeon General on the health risks of cigarette smoking is stated on every pack of cigarettes.

TV researcher Dr. Leonard Eron of the University of Michigan has said, "The only people who dispute the connection between smoking and cancer are people in the tobacco industry. And the only people who dispute the TV and violence connection are people in the entertainment industry."

In one of many hearings on the topic, former US Surgeon General Dr. Jesse Steinfeld testified before the US Senate on his assessment of the research on TV violence and behavior:

> It is clear to me that the causal relationship between televised violence and antisocial behavior is sufficient to warrant appropriate and immediate remedial action...But there comes a time when the data are sufficient to justify action. That time has come.

Steinfeld made that statement in 1972, more than 20 years ago. But the "remedial action" he spoke of did not come to pass. In fact, as channels have proliferated, violence on TV has become even more graphic and more pervasive.

More recently, an American Psychological Association (APA) task force examined the plethora of research on the issue. Its chair, Dr. Aletha C. Huston, professor of human development and psychology at the University of Kansas, said to a congressional committee in 1988, "Virtually all independent scholars agree that there is evidence that television can cause aggressive behavior."

The "Vast Wasteland" Has Gotten Vaster

The first person to call TV a "vast wasteland" was Newton Minow, the activist Federal Communications Commission Chairman under President Kennedy in 1961. In
a now famous speech to the National Association of
Broadcasters, he said:

> When television is good, nothing—not the theater, not
> the magazines or newspapers—is better. But when televi-
> sion is bad, nothing is worse. I invite you to sit down in
> front of your television set when your station goes on the
> air and stay there without a book, magazine, newspaper,
> profit-and-loss sheet, or rating book to distract you—and
> keep your eyes glued to that set until the station signs
> off. I can assure you that you will observe a vast waste-
> land.
>
> You will see a procession of game shows, violence,
> audience participation shows, formula comedies about
> totally unbelievable families, blood and thunder, may-
> hem, violence, sadism, murder, western badmen, west-
> ern good men, private eyes, gangsters, more violence,
> and cartoons. And, endlessly, commercials—many
> screaming, cajoling, and offending. And most of all,
> boredom. True, you will see a few things you will enjoy.
> But they will be very, very few. And if you think I exag-
> gerate, try it.

Thirty years and countless new channels later, Minow
hasn't changed his mind. In a speech entitled, "How Vast
the Wasteland Now," he said:

> In 1961 I worried that my children would not benefit
> much from television, but in 1991 I worry that my
> grandchildren will actually be harmed by it. In 1961 they
> didn't make PG-13 movies, much less NC-17. Now a six-
> year-old can watch them on cable.

The US Surgeon General's Office and the APA are joined by the National Institutes of Mental Health and the Centers for Disease Control in this conclusion: There is a direct relationship between televised violence and violent behavior.

In plain language, WATCHING TV VIOLENCE CAN BE HARMFUL TO YOUR CHILD'S HEALTH. Like the cigarette warning, those 10 words should be printed in bold, black letters on the side of every TV set sold in this country. Since Congress won't do it, broadcasters won't do it, and TV manufacturers won't do it, I suggest you do it for yourself and for your children. Make a sign and tape it to the side of your TV set, as a daily reminder before you light up—the screen.

> "The anecdotal evidence is often more compelling than the scientific studies. Ask any homicide cop from London to Los Angeles to Bangkok if TV violence induces real-life violence and listen carefully to the cynical, knowing laugh.... Ask Sergeant John O'Malley of the New York Police Department about a nine-year-old boy who sprayed a Bronx office building with gunfire. The boy explained to the astonished sergeant how he learned to load his Uzi-like firearm: 'I watch a lot of TV.'"
> —Journalist Carl Cannon, writing in *Mother Jones*

Take Up Arms Against TV Violence

Here are some tactics you can use to combat TV violence at home:

- **Minimize it.** TV violence takes many forms, so you should decide which forms you'll permit, and at what age. If your child likes to watch cartoons, for instance, it will be difficult to

The Measurable Effects of Watching TV Violence

University of Michigan psychologists Dr. Leonard Eron and Dr. Rowell Huesmann have followed the viewing habits of a group of children for decades. They found that watching violence on television is the single factor most closely associated with aggressive behavior—more than poverty, race, or parental behavior.

In 1960, Eron embarked on a landmark longitudinal study of over 800 eight-year-olds. He found that children who watched many hours of violent television tended to be more aggressive in the playground and the classroom.

Eron and Huesmann checked back with these students 11 and 22 years later and found that the aggressive eight-year-olds grew up to become even more aggressive 19- and 30-year-olds, with greater troubles—including domestic violence and more traffic tickets—than their less aggressive counterparts who did not watch as much television. And the researchers found that *even if a child is not aggressive at the age of eight, but watches substantial amounts of violent programming, he will be more aggressive at 19 than his peers who didn't watch violent TV.*

In Eron and Huesmann's testimony before Congress in 1992, they said: "Television violence affects youngsters of all ages, of both genders, at all socioeconomic levels and all levels of intelligence. The effect is not limited to children who are already disposed to being aggressive and is not restricted to this country."

eradicate every instance of the Pink Panther running into a brick wall or King Arthur's knights vanquishing the enemy with their swords. However, more true-to-life violence, on TV movies, dramas, and "reality shows," can disturb younger children, as well as glorify shootings, stabbings, and car chases for older children. Agree with your children to eliminate such programs.

- **Defuse it.** When your children watch violent acts on TV, even in seemingly innocuous cartoon shows, ensure that they understand your opinion about violence. Discuss other ways in which disputes can be resolved, using examples from your own as well as your child's life. When you believe your child is ready, relate experiences you or family members may have had with violence in your own lives.

- **Analyze it.** Discuss how the violence in shows does not resemble violence in real life, how stunt performers simulate brawls and gunfights. When your child is ready, you might point out the human toll of real violence, perhaps by citing individuals you may see injured in car accidents or at hospitals. Help your child become more critical of how TV violence is manufactured for his viewing. Engage him in the question, "Why do you think there is violence on TV?"

"The Mind Is Like a Filing Cabinet"

The clearest explanation I have heard of the effects of TV violence on behavior comes not from a social science researcher but from a 23-year-old man named Sherman Spears. Four years ago, he was shot in an Oakland housing project and paralyzed from the waist down.

I met him at a conference on youth violence. From his wheelchair, Spears was describing his project, Teens on Target, where teens counsel other teens about alternatives to violence and visit hospital trauma centers to dissuade young victims of shootings and stabbings from retaliation. I asked him whether he thought there was any relationship between TV violence and young people committing violent crime.

"I look at it like this," Spears said. "The mind is like a filing cabinet. Everything you see and do goes into a file in that filing cabinet. And when something happens to you, you go to that file."

HONEY, I SOLD THE KIDS: TV AND ADVERTISING

Around the age of five, our daughter, Maggie, started watching more commercial TV and reciting commercial jingles, songs, and slogans. One Sunday morning, we were looking for a place to go out for breakfast. Maggie, who typically chooses McDonald's, said she wanted to go to "IHOP." This was new. She had never asked to go there before. Intrigued, Ruth and I asked her why and what "IHOP" stood for.

"It's the International House of Pancakes," Maggie responded. "You can have the Fruity Country Griddle Cakes for just $3.99." She had memorized the pitch line, word for word, from a commercial that morning. Guess where we headed?

Recently, we were talking about losing weight. Maggie offered, "Why don't you use Nestlé's Sweet Success? That lady on TV, who did it for three weeks, lost six pounds. You have a shake for breakfast, a shake for lunch, and special chewy healthy bars for snacks. It's your favorite, 'cause it's chocolate. And then you can have a sensible dinner." Almost verbatim from the commercial. Now I'm wondering whether I should try it.

> The average American child watches 20,000 commercials a year. Advertisers spend about $700 million annually advertising to kids.

Kids Are an Advertiser's Best Friends

As the advertising world knows so well, television is a medium made for selling. Ad execs should be especially thankful for small children, because they work so hard for them. Most parents can recount similar instances when a child recited a fast-food special or a company's slogan with startling accuracy. Commercial jingles are among the songs we sing with our children.

My family's excursion to IHOP will come as no surprise to advertisers. Their ads for toys, sugared cereal, and fast food frequently interrupt kids' shows for a reason. They know that kids wield a lot of influence on the family pocketbook. Even though producers, researchers, policymakers, educators, and parents may not agree on much about television, they can agree on one thing: TV advertising works.

> When Philo T. Farnsworth, the inventor of television, tested his first American broadcast, the first image he transmitted was the dollar sign.

Watching the Most Commercial TV in the World

The United States has arguably the most commercialized system of media in the world. American TV mainly exists to sell audiences to advertisers. Its main purpose is not to deliver entertaining shows to viewers but to use the popularity of programs to bring viewers to advertising messages. The commercial TV shows we watch are merely "the bait" to attract us to the commercials.

Advertising takes up 60 percent of newspapers, 17 percent of network prime time, and 27 percent of other network time, says Leo Bogart, a former advertising executive, in his incisive paper, "The American Media System and Its Commercial Culture." Advertising messages, he writes, "tell us to consume, right now, right away, [and] teach us to take pride in outward appearances. There is a strong veneration of inanimate objects; they are endowed with the ability to arouse levels of emotional affect that most human beings normally feel toward each other."

If there is a way to use television to move inanimate products off shelves, media marketers will find it. In the new genre of "infomercials," it is difficult to tell where the commercial leaves off and where the program begins.

The Home Shopping Network is a natural extension of the media urge to sell. Beyond merely advertising products, the channel becomes the call-in superstore, open 24 hours a day; all you need is a credit card.

Will expanded channels and new interactive capabilities bring our children new educational opportunities? While it is too soon to tell, I'm confident that these interactive channels will accomplish one goal: devising new and even more devious ways to sell products to our children, and through them, to ourselves.

Make It a Light, Bud?

A group of University of California, Berkeley, researchers surveyed 468 fifth- and sixth-graders and found that frequent TV sports viewers recognized beer commercials, brands, and slogans. Those who paid the most attention to the commercials felt that drinking beer was "cool" and expect to drink as adults. And 88 percent of the children studied could identify Spuds Mackenzie and his connection to Bud Light.

67 percent of adults can identify Joe Camel; 91 percent of six-year-olds can.

TV Sells Without Even Trying

As parents, we must also understand that popular TV characters, because of their celebrity, are TV billboards for their own product tie-ins. Since the mid 1970s, there has been a rule against the blatant shilling of products during the show by the human hosts, puppets, or cartoon characters that children know and love.

But manufacturers of children's products, from books to blue jeans to bed sheets, understand that the presence of well-known characters on the air is enough. From G.I. Joe to Strawberry Brite to Barney, even the smallest child, while going down the toy store aisle in a shopping cart, will stop and badger his parents at the sight of his favorite character as a plush toy or on a toy box.

96 percent of the food ads on children's television are for sugared cereals, candy, cookies, and junk food.

It Looked Better on TV!

While we can't change Maggie's penchant for spouting ad copy, Ruth and I can help her watch commercials with a more critical eye. Once kids reach school age and can discriminate between shows and commercials, becoming savvy commercial critics can be both empowering and fun. With their finely honed sense of fairness, children can become outraged at less-than-honest commercials.

Here are some quick tips for helping to defend your children against TV ads:

• **Mute the ads.** A commercial loses a lot of its magnetism when there's no sound. If your kids are watching commercial television, hand over the remote and teach them how to silence commercials with the mute button. Make "muting" a condition of watching commercial TV: "When the commercials are on, the sound is off."

• **Fast-forward the ads.** If you tape commercial programs, you can fast-forward through the commercials. By renting or buying videocassettes, you can bypass the commercial problem altogether.

• **Critique the ads.** Seize the opportunity to teach your children some media literacy tips. During commercials ask them: How did the advertisers sell their product—and make you want to buy it? Did it make the product look better than it really is?

How? What if there was no music in the commercial? What is the real message behind the ad—that you'll be happier or have more friends if you buy the product? By looking at the packaging of the advertisement, as well as its true message—more friends, more fun, more glamour—you can help your child learn to "read" and "counter-argue" commercials.

- **See through the ads.** Give your child a behind-the-scenes look at the making of commercials. Consumers Union, publishers of *Consumer Reports*, publishes an excellent children's magazine, *Zillions*, to help kids become smarter consumers by taking a critical look at the advertising industry. In addition, *Consumer Reports* has produced several videos—including *Buy Me That: A Kid's Survival Guide to Advertising* and *Buy Me That, Too!*—which have been broadcast on HBO. In these videos, kids get a look at the tricks and gimmicks advertisers use to lure viewers to buy. You and your child will gain insights into how TV ads are themselves manufactured products.

"Once, when I was brushing my four-year-old daughter's hair, she said, 'My hair isn't pretty and shiny.' She has beautiful long, soft, blond hair. I said, 'Nicky, your hair is beautiful!' She said, 'It's not like the lady's in the shampoo commercial.' Imagine a four-year-old feeling insecure because of a TV commercial! So we don't watch commercial TV anymore."

—*Diane, mother of a daughter, 4*

TELEVISION'S JAUNDICED EYE: RACE AND GENDER STEREOTYPING

Stereotyping is actually one of the ways in which children learn. Young children need to make sense of a complex world, to simplify it, to put things into categories, and attach predictable traits to them. Much of a preschooler's learning involves mastering the "scripts" of daily life, and the rules and regularities of human activities. For instance, it is very useful for a preschooler to have a "stereotype" of his childcare center. It's comforting to know that circle time comes first, then outdoor play, then snack time, then art activity.

But while it may be valuable to teach your child the ways in which the world is regular and predictable, the message we aim to teach regarding human beings is quite different: that each person should be regarded as an individual, and valued for who they are, not their color, sex, physical appearance, sexual preference, country of origin, or any other categorization used by adults.

This isn't easy—for adults or children—because we receive so many messages to the contrary. Schools, the media, and our own families all conspire to give children the impression that certain kinds of people can be assumed to behave in certain ways.

Too often, from an early age, children acquire stereotypes of how girls and boys are supposed to behave, or what Asian-Americans, African-Americans, Native Americans, older people, or disabled people are like. Even supposedly positive stereotypes— Asians are good at math and science, girls are good at reading— imply that these groups don't have to be or aren't good at other things. Perhaps the most insidious danger of stereotypes is that they deny the many similarities among us and the humanity of all people.

TV's Characters: The Good, the Bad, and the Ugly

Television has enormous power to invent and perpetuate certain racial, sexual, and other stereotypes, through both its programming and its commercials. Dr. George Gerbner, of the University of Pennsylvania's Annenberg School of Communications, explains that these broadcast images serve as "cultural indicators" of key power relationships and values in our society. Consider the shows your family watches. Which groups are portrayed as powerful, successful, and competent? Which are presented as weak, dispossessed, and dependent?

TV is defining for our families and society what power and success mean. Because of TV's commercial motives, if violence sells, someone's got to be the bad guy. If sex sells, someone's got to be sexy. If stupidity sells, someone's got to be stupid.

The annals of television research are filled with studies of stereotyping on TV. The American Psychological Association's Task Force on Television and Society reviewed these studies and concluded: "Each of the five groups discussed—children, elderly people, minorities, women, and gays and lesbians—are often underrepresented or portrayed in narrow, stereotyped roles on television. Their low social status and relatively low value as a market for advertising both probably contribute to these patterns of television portrayals."

In the following two chapters, we'll look at some pernicious stereotypes and also some ways to avoid, as well as to use, these problematic portrayals in educating your children.

Rerunning TV's Racial Stereotypes

Many African-American parents interviewed in KQED Parents Project focus groups said they are offended by commercial TV's heavy portrayal of African-Americans as criminals or victims of crime. They did not see themselves or their children reflected in TV's families. As one father said, "Stereotyped roles on TV give us no justice, do not show our strengths and diversity, and who we are as a people."

> "We watch *Martin*. It's not the best show for kids, but as a black family, we feel it's important for the kids to see blacks on TV. When my daughter would see black men walking down the street she would get excited and afraid. She thought they were violent or drug dealers. She got that from TV."
> —*Pam, mother of two daughters, 5 and 11, and a son, 7*

There have been some positive efforts to escape television's stereotypes of African-Americans, such as *The Cosby Show* and, more recently, *Roc*. But these attempts, worthy as they are, can't compensate for the vast number of offensive, stereotyped portrayals, many of which have been brought back in reruns.

The Big Problem with Television's "Heritage"

These older programs showcase old attitudes best left in the archives. It is frightening to realize that as the number of cable channels increase, every series produced in the history of TV has a chance of being rerun over and over again. As these shows come back, their stereotypes, like ghosts from decades past, reappear in programs our children watch.

For example, Nickelodeon's evening schedule includes reruns of shows from the 1960s and '70s—*I Love Lucy*, *The Bob Newhart Show*, *The Mary Tyler Moore Show*, *Bullwinkle*, *Superman*, *The Partridge Family*, *Dragnet*, and *Get Smart*. Nick at Night's on-air motto, "Preserving Television's Heritage," deserves a closer look. In these old shows, there is a marked absence of major roles for people of color.

Some characters that do appear are better forgotten. In *Get Smart*, Maxwell Smart vanquishes an Asian CHAOS agent who cannot pronounce his L's and R's. When that cartoon canine, Mr. Peabody, and his boy sidekick, Sherman, travel in their Way-Back Machine to China, they encounter a bumbling Confucius and a slant-eyed Genghis Khan, speaking in fake, thick Chinese accents. After Maggie saw this episode, I asked her what she thought of it. "Chinese people don't look like this," she said, and pulled back her eyelids, a racist gesture I remember from my childhood.

These shows are from an era when caricatures of racial groups were thought by some to be funny. However, racism and sexism are not a "heritage" worth "preserving."

Meanwhile, teachers and parents are by no means immune from being targeted by commercial TV stereotypes. On the children's TV landscape, parents, grandparents, and teachers who have genuine, caring relationships with children are an endangered species.

Immunize Your Child Against TV's Stereotypes

Inoculate your child against TV's stereotypes by identifying them when you find them, counter-arguing against them, and refusing to apply them in real life. Many children may not note the negative messages carried by certain characters. They may simply find them funny or entertaining. Here are some specific tips:

- **Limit your child's exposure.** The fewer negative stereotypes your child sees, the better. Even if your child is watching just a few hours of commercial TV a week, she'll be exposed to obvious as well as subtle stereotypes on programs and ads.
- **Look closely at the characters your child sees.** What messages do they send concerning race, gender, and roles? Voice your disapproval of stereotyped characters and why you disapprove. Help him understand that reruns recreate older stereotypes. Give examples of people you know who destroy the stereotypes, in your family, your community, and throughout history.
- **Critique other media.** Look at the ads in newspapers, magazines, and billboards for cars, cigarettes, and liquor. Talk about how the product is glamorized and which audiences are targeted.

In this age of ethnic marketing, talk about how ethnic groups are linked to certain products and services. Pay attention to stereo-types in children's books and movies. Do princesses always need to win the affection of a prince? Do all Asians know karate?

• **Find programs that counter stereotypes.** As much as TV can stereotype human beings, it can also do precisely the oppo-site and help your child appreciate human diversity. In Part IV, I'll discuss some shows that help tear down stereotypes and raise a new awareness of the races and the sexes.

DON'T LET YOUR GIRLS GROW UP TO BE BARBIES

In best-sellers, women tell men *You Just Don't Understand*, perhaps because *Men Are from Mars, Women Are from Venus*. Men and women come from different cultures, maybe different planets, and definitely speak different languages.

No wonder. Even today, boys and girls are largely raised in separate cultures. This segregation by sex actually starts at birth, when parents dress newborn girls in pink and boys in blue. (When Maggie was a baby, I used to dress her up in blue just to see what would happen. Invariably, people exclaimed: "What a beautiful boy!")

Teachers, parents, and the media often conspire to cast boys and girls in stereotyped roles. One of the greatest challenges for parents is to fight this conspiracy. But as long as some parents and teachers continue to believe in sex differences, they will continue to give preferential treatment to boys in science and mathematics and to girls in reading and art.

I find this pattern disturbing, especially since much of my career has been devoted to encouraging girls and boys to cross society's gender boundaries. I researched and wrote my doctoral dissertation on gender differences in the use of computers. Two shows on which I worked, *3-2-1 Contact* and *Square One TV*, specifically set out to encourage girls' interests in science and mathematics. In Part IV, I'll discuss ways in which positive, counter-stereotyped portrayals can help your daughter see that she can be a scientist, and your son an artist.

Gender Inequity in the Classroom and on the TV Screen

The inequalities boys and girls face in the classroom are well documented. In 1992, the American Association of University Women (AAUW) published a much-quoted report on how girls are shortchanged in the educational process and how boys are called on more often in class, thus benefiting from greater support from parents and teachers.

For more than three decades, researchers such as Carol Gilligan at the Harvard Graduate School of Education and Myra and David Sadker of American University have studied gender differences in socialization. Gilligan has documented how girls, usually confident, independent, and spirited in their younger years, lose their "voice" and their self-confidence and become unsure and dependent in adolescence.

Much of popular TV programming aids and abets this conspiracy. Many TV series reinforce a distorted view of male and female roles and relationships between the sexes. In the TV world, the ways that males and females talk, dress, behave, and interact often follow a stereotypical script.

Several years ago, there was no children's program on a commercial network with a lead female character, not even a She-Ra, Princess of Power. Why? Simple. Research with children showed that while girls would watch programs with both male and female characters, boys were distinctly put off by shows with lead female characters.

In order to maximize audiences, therefore, programmers decided to eliminate female lead characters altogether. In the calculus of commercial programming, redressing gender inequities hardly figures in.

The Problem with Reruns Redux

Kids' shows aren't the only ones affected—other programs are afflicted with stereotypes, too. Children between the ages of eight and 12 mostly watch shows produced for teens and adults—sitcoms, game shows, movies, music videos, and others.

And thanks to expanded channels and TV's voracious appetite for reruns, programs from the 1960s through the 1980s are back and are viewed by large audiences of children. But do these shows present the types of male and female characters we'd like our children to see? In many popular shows from those years— *Mission Impossible, Get Smart, The Man from U.N.C.L.E.,* to name a few—many women's roles were primarily as young, romantic appendages for men.

One study of women appearing in TV shows from the late 1970s concluded: "The model female on television is a young adult, beautiful, dependent, helpless, passive, concerned with interpersonal relations, warm, and valued for her appearance rather than for her capabilities and competencies, personal and professional."

I Dream of Jeannie, while it may have been a comedy hit in its time, features a scantily clad female "genie" whose sole purpose is to serve her master, an astronaut. In an *I Love Lucy* episode, Lucy and Ethel go for job interviews but are at a loss to describe any skills to the male interviewer. Even Fred Flintstone and Barney Rubble get to have all the fun, while Wilma and Betty stay home to tend the fire. Thanks to the rerun, these stereotyped women from our own childhoods have been given a new lease on life.

> In a typical TV season, the average adolescent watches 14,000 acts of sexual contact or innuendo in television programs and ads, according to a 1992 Planned Parenthood study.

Prime Time Today: More Women's Roles, More Sex

In recent years, women's roles in prime-time shows have become much more diverse and interesting. Women play complex, competent, and authoritative roles in shows such as *Murphy Brown*, *The Golden Girls*, *Northern Exposure*, and *L. A. Law*. Compare the women in those shows to female characters in *Three's Company* or *I Dream of Jeannie*.

However, this positive trend coincides with a rise in sexuality as a major theme in programs and commercials that children watch. The lurid story lines of soap operas—love triangles, rape, incest, and infidelity—have escaped their daytime schedules and are now firmly entrenched in prime-time programs watched by much younger people.

In 1988, the American Academy of Pediatrics noted that 75 percent of music videos showed sexually suggestive material; 56 percent portrayed violent acts, usually directed toward women.

Modern Fairy Tales: The Prince and Princess Do More Than Kiss

Sex vies with violence as the major theme of TV in the 1990s. Commercials such as the one featuring young men whose choice of a beer is rewarded with a bevy of beauties in swimsuits are common; as if turnabout were fair play, another ad features women in an office building ogling a handsome construction worker drinking a diet soda.

In many of the most popular TV shows, it seems that the main reason for getting to know a person of the opposite sex is to have sex with them. The popular *Beverly Hills 90210* and *Melrose Place* emphasize physical beauty and sexuality as the center of relationships between young men and women. The stars of these shows are featured everywhere, from fan-magazine covers to talk shows. For many children, they are the romantic icons of the nineties.

You can battle these stereotypes using the same techniques discussed in the previous chapter.

A LOOK ABROAD:
THERE IS A
BETTER WAY

Plainly stated, American television does not serve the educational needs of our children in any planned or comprehensive way. There has been a chronic shortage of funding and commitment in this country to create high-quality programming for children and teens.

In 1991, federal spending for public broadcasting was about $1 per person in the US. Japan spent about $17 per person, Canada $32, and Great Britain $38.

An Olympics of Children's Television

There is a better way. Other nations in Europe and Asia as well as Australia do a much better job of serving their child audiences.

Every two years in Munich, the best children's TV series are honored in the Prix Jeunesse (Youth Prize), an international competitive festival of children's television. Hundreds of producers, broadcasters, researchers, and educators from around the world gather to judge the entries. It is the Olympics of children's TV.

A look at some innovative programs from the Prix Jeunesse gives a glimpse of the different philosophies and approaches to children's programming around the world. The winners demonstrate a much richer use of television than we Americans have imagined. Our children have never been treated to the inspiring dramas, thoughtful documentaries, and other creative uses of the TV medium, such as the following:

• *The Boy Who Called the Cows Home* tells the story of a young Tibetan boy who tends the cows for his family's farm. A school is built near the boy's home, and he starts to attend, although his father is dubious about the value of schooling.

• *Beat That*, produced by Channel 4 in England, enables young people to tell their own story. In one program, disabled and able-bodied youngsters organize a restaurant.

• *Babel Tower*, from Poland, features Polish and German children who must find ways to communicate across their language barrier. They do so through a series of games, which spark enjoyment and cooperation.

• *Moskito*, from Germany, addresses the racism that has plagued Berlin in recent years. Through documentaries, home-made music videos, comedic sketches, cartoons, and a studio confrontation, immigrants and skinheads show the damaging effects of racism.

If we really cared about the television our children see, we would seek to create full-service children's channels that offer a microcosm of adult programming. The British Broadcasting Corporation (BBC) probably comes the closest to doing so. As Anna Home, head of BBC Children's Programs, says, "BBC children's programming reflects the range found in the adult schedule—it includes drama, news, comedy, entertainment, nature programs, documentaries. It is educative in the broadest sense."

A few American programs have won the Prix Jeunesse over the years, such as *Sesame Street* and *Reading Rainbow*. But like the Olympic event of ice hockey, the number of American winners are few and far between. In the international arena of children's TV, we Americans simply can't compete.

Lessons from the Prix Jeunesse

Dr. Edward Palmer describes these themes from some Prix Jeunesse winners:

> The quest for beauty, the strength to right a wrong, the will to prevail in the name of justice and fair play, the tenacity to remain courageous in the face of obstacles and to persist in making a wonderful dream into reality; to see and respect perspectives which differ from one's own;...to be self-reliant and resourceful; to find one's place among family and friends; to observe well—for pleasure, learning, and understanding; and to become aware that, whatever problem or hurt one may experience, there are others who have known it, shared it, and cared about it.

Any parent reading these themes will recognize them as values we want to convey to our children.

The Myth of American Public Television

American underachievement in children's television should come as no surprise in light of the minimal funding provided in the US.

In Great Britain, every household pays an annual "broadcast license fee" to support the BBC. This year, the fee is $122, generating $2 billion for the BBC. In Japan and Sweden, households paid $294 and $185, respectively. At the same time, the US Congress appropriated only about $300 million to pay for public broadcasting—or about $3 per household.

On a per capita basis, the Parliament of Great Britain commits almost *40 times* to public broadcasting what our Congress does. In children's programming alone, in a country with one-fifth the population of ours, the BBC spends about $80 million a year, compared with $16 million spent by PBS.

We really can't compete with the quality of other countries' children's television without a stronger funding mechanism for public TV. Unless some creative solutions are found to provide a much higher level of funding for educational children's programs, children's TV in the US will continue to languish and fall far short of a comprehensive educational service for our children.

RAISE YOUR VOICE TO IMPROVE CHILDREN'S TELEVISION

Lately, we've read about debates surrounding TV violence in the newspaper, but we rarely hear about any real changes. All the hearings, conferences, legal filings, research studies, and legislative proposals haven't led to much improvement in what our children see on the screen. This is a tale of the decades-long clash between TV networks and the Federal Communications Commission, of legal wranglings and bureaucratic wrestling, of a nation's ambivalence about the television our kids watch.

In the past year, leaders in Washington, including President Clinton, have voiced concern over the effects of TV violence on young people, and legislators have rattled the saber of stricter regulations over broadcasters. Leaders from the broadcasting and cable television industry, hat in hand, have offered to police themselves, but they also assert their First Amendment rights to free speech and to broadcast as they please. A proposal by

Representative Edward Markey to manufacture a "V-chip" in TV sets, enabling parents to block out violent programs, has been met with outcries over censorship.

Meanwhile, precious years of a child's life—or entire childhoods—pass by. The moral of this story is: Don't wait for Washington. We must act first to control TV in our own homes.

> "Children's programming on commercial broadcast television remains the video equivalent of a Twinkie— kids enjoy it despite the absolute absence of any nutritional content."
> —*Rep. Edward Markey of Massachusetts, Chairman, US House of Representatives Telecommunications Subcommittee and cosponsor of the Children's Television Act of 1990*

TV: A Toaster with Pictures? Not!

In the 1980s, the Reagan Administration's policy of deregulating businesses was also applied to television. For more than a decade, the Federal government took the same stance on the TV industry that it took with other industries.

Former FCC Chairman Mark Fowler signaled this new attitude in 1981: "Under the coming marketplace approach, the commission should, so far as possible, defer to a broadcaster's judgment about how best to compete for viewers and listeners, because this serves the public interest." In a now-famous analogy, Fowler stated: "Television is an appliance, like a toaster, only with pictures."

The deregulation of television opened up a virtual free-for-all, wherein programs could be produced and aired without regard for levels of violence, sexual portrayals, stereotyping, or any other content issue. The regulatory gloves were off. Today's children are still paying the price.

> "I'm the grandmother of the Children's Television Act. I should have been the mother, but it took 25 years."
> —*Peggy Charren, founder of Action for Children's Television*

Fred Flintstone Teaching Paleontology?
Commercial Stations Respond

After years of hearings, debate, and lobbying by public interest groups, spearheaded by Action for Children's Television, Congress passed the Children's Television Act of 1990. The Act mandated that all FCC-licensed TV stations must broadcast some educational TV programming. To renew their licenses, stations must show that broadcasts truly meet the educational needs of children.

A year later, it was clear that some commercial stations were absent from class that day the rest of us learned what the word "educational" means. A station in Detroit submitted *Super Mario Brothers 4* as meeting the mandate, with the justification that "Yoshi learns to have more self-confidence." *Yo, Yogi!* taught children this lesson: "Snag learns that he can capture the bank-robbing cockroach more successfully by using his head, rather than his muscles."

Here is the crossroads where politics, commerce, and the interests of children meet. And commerce continues to win out,
because stations can always buy older cartoon shows for a frac-
tion of the cost of producing new educational children's programs. While some stations have taken the Children's Television
Act seriously, looking for newer and better children's programs, it
is not yet clear what recourse the FCC will take to put real bite
into the act.

> "Televisions don't shoot people, guns do. I can't remem-
> ber the last time, or the first time, that somebody com-
> plained to me about violence on this television station."
> —*A president of a commercial television station affiliate*

Looking for a Leader

Few heads of commercial TV networks or production companies
have been willing to take a stand on TV violence. Instead, industry leaders have dug in their heels and been dragged to confront
the issue. A growing number of TV station managers already
agree their programming is too violent, yet the network response
—to run viewer advisories before extremely violent programs—
is a most tepid form of "self-regulation."

One of the few industry leaders who has been willing to take a
stand is Ted Turner. In his 1993 testimony before Congress, he
admitted that his own cable network, Turner Network Television,
showed more violent programs than he would like. "[W]e are
being forced to by the competition. They're guilty of murder. We
all are—me, too," he said.

Turner acknowledged that the entertainment industry would do little unless forced by Congress. "Unless you keep the gun pointed at their heads, all you'll get is mumbly, mealy-mouthed BS. They just hope the subject will go away."

Let Ted Turner and the "silent majority" in commercial TV know if you agree. Write to your local TV station managers and the heads of networks and let them know that viewer advisories are not enough. Better programming is what the Children's Television Act is all about.

> "Once I thought the most important political statement we could make about television was to turn it off. But television can instruct, inform, and inspire, as well as distract, distort, and demean. And turning it off rejects the good with the bad. My family wants its voice added to the summons for quality, and I urge you to speak up, too, in every way possible. This marvelous medium, with all its potential for laughter and light, is worth fighting for."
>
> —*Bill Moyers*

Changing the Channel Isn't Enough

Viewer advisories and V-chips only deal with controlling what is already on the air. In the end, our children deserve better programming. But if, in the FCC's eyes, *Super Mario Brothers 4* meets the educational mandate, then laws to encourage better children's television will also not achieve that goal.

There have been some positive results from the Children's Television Act. In 1992, a number of new children's series were commissioned, including ABC's *Beakman's World* and *Bill Nye, The Science Guy*, on commercial stations and PBS. "Most of the alternatives to comic book nonsense are a direct result of the Children's Television Act," says Peggy Charren, ACT's former president. "But the best hope for real improvement in children's television is a well-funded and publicly supported children's TV service."

I agree. With a publicly funded service, writers and producers can afford to take risks and experiment with new program topics and forms that would be canceled if not quickly profitable for a commercial network. Most innovative Prix Jeunesse winners from around the world are produced by publicly funded broadcasters in Europe and Asia.

> According to a 1993 survey by *Electronic Media* magazine, 74 percent of TV station managers agree that TV is too violent. The majority favor voluntary network reduction in the violence and the placing of warning labels on the most violent shows.

The Underfunding of Educational Children's Television

What public TV offers today is not nearly what a "well funded, publicly supported children's TV service" should offer. Substantially more funding will be needed for a more comprehensive educational TV service for children, in expanding programming, promotion, and outreach with parents and teachers.

Public funding for children's television continues to decline. As part of the Children's Television Act, a National Endowment for Children's Educational Television was established to provide additional funding for children's TV. In 1993, $3 million was awarded. In 1994, the funding was cut to $1 million. These sums are hardly enough to pay for part of one major TV series.

In his 1988 book, *Television and America's Children,* Dr. Edward Palmer, an international consultant on educational media, estimated that a national educational children's service would cost $60 million per year.

While this level of funding is well within reach of our federal budgets, it could be provided without any additional federal spending. It only requires a different view of where the profits from commercial television and advertising should go.

Other sectors of our economy, such as farmers grazing their herds, mining companies extracting precious metals, and oil companies drilling for oil on public lands, pay fees back to the public treasury for the opportunity to generate private profits.

Commercial broadcasters and advertisers also use public property—the airwaves—to derive their profits. It makes sense to require those who profit from our public airwaves to devote a small percentage of their revenue to serving the public interest. An innovative and robust noncommercial educational service for children could easily be funded by levying a small fee on the profits commercial broadcasters make by "renting" our public property, the airwaves.

This concept of a "broadcast spectrum fee" has been raised before. But it's worth keeping the principle in mind, as we approach a new age of expanded channels and interactive services.

Making a Difference Outside Your Home

While we can control what our children watch, we can't improve
their broadcast choices with our remote controls. We also need to
raise our voices to help bring about better children's programming. While this book is primarily about taking action at home
to manage and use television, you can make a difference outside
your home, too. The Children's Television Act reflects what active
parents' groups can do (see Peggy Charren's call to action in the
Preface on page xi). Here are three steps parents can take to make
our voices heard and to keep children's television on the public
agenda:

• **Voice your opinions to broadcasters and cablecasters.**
Write to your congressional representatives and the FCC, and let
them know you are concerned about children's television and
want to see the Children's Television Act enforced. (You'll find
addresses of advocacy groups, television companies, and government agencies in the Resource Guide.)

• **Monitor what's going on in children's television**. You've
already made a commitment by reading this book. Continue to
look for newspaper and magazine reports on FCC action regarding the Children's Television Act, as well as new children's TV initiatives. Consider joining one of the children's media advocacy
groups listed in the Resource Guide.

• **Organize a parent education session at your childcare
facility or school**. Share your knowledge with other parents
informally, as well as through parents' nights at your local school
or childcare center. Invite speakers from commercial, cable, and
PBS channels to discuss their programming and future plans.

Meanwhile, parents with young children can't wait for a powerful industry to change, or for Congress and the FCC to make new rules and designate new funding for educational programming. Once again, the responsibility falls to parents to provide for our children's welfare. We'll have to shoulder more of the burden to find and use educational programs with our children and to make the best use of the medium we can. As with all matters of child-rearing, regulation of TV must start at home. That's what Part III is all about.

Taking Control
of the Set

INTELLIGENT TELEVISION: FROM UNCONSCIOUS TO CONSCIOUS VIEWING

So much of how we raise our children tends to be unconscious. As many parents admit, we're making it up as we go along. Or, we resort to our most familiar models, our own parents. We parent as we were parented.

But our parenting doesn't have to be unconscious. By reading books, talking to others, and reflecting on our parenting styles, we can seek to become conscious parents. We can become aware of how our behavior and language constantly send overt and covert messages to our children.

Most TV watching tends to be unplanned and unconscious as well. When we have some free time, we plop down on the couch and click on the TV set. In many families, the TV is turned on as soon as a member of the family wakes up or enters the house, whether anyone is watching or not. The TV becomes almost like a radio, an appliance playing video Muzak while family members walk in and out of rooms, go back and forth to the refrigerator, and chat on the phone. Like bad wallpaper, it's there every day.

> In the average American home with children, the television is on nearly 60 hours a week, or 8.5 hours a day. In single-person homes, the set is on an average 40 hours a week, nearly 6 hours a day.

On All the Time

The Television Viewing Lab at WGBH-Boston confirms that watching the TV is only one of many things people do while the set is on. In the lab's simulated living room, complete with a large color TV, remote control, a comfortable couch, magazines, and snacks, volunteers "watch" TV. Repeatedly, they also read, eat, converse, and even doze off. This scene—whether in a lab or a living room—is not exactly the picture of rapt attention that would make an advertiser's heart soar.

And, all too often, parents don't get involved in what their children watch. A study by Dr. Howard Taras and other pediatricians at the University of California found that 85 percent of parents with children ages three to eight did not guide their children's program selections, and two-thirds of the parents surveyed did not discuss programs with their children frequently and used television primarily to entertain their children.

If you watch the average amount of television—4 hours a day, 28 hours a week, for both American children and adults—you will spend 13 years watching TV by the time you're 75.

Making TV a Choice, Not a Habit

What can you do if your family uses TV in desultory, habitual, and unconscious ways? The trick is to make TV watching a conscious activity. Make turning on the TV something children elect to do, rather than the one choice they make when they're not doing something else.

But keep in mind that this trick includes you as a parent. It won't work if you tell your kids that they have to select programs consciously and they see you lounging casually in front of the set for hours. Children do as children see.

You can begin to change the ways your children use TV by entering into a simple series of dialogues with them:

- **Change their patterns.** If your children want to watch TV, have them ask you first. Just as they ask you if they can go out and play, agree that they must ask you if they can watch TV.
- **Answer—with questions.** Don't just answer yes or no; ask your children "What do you want to watch? What's on? How about watching a video you've rented or recorded?" Ask them if there's something else they've been thinking of doing, like reading or playing outside.

- **Ask yourself some questions.** Is there some other activity that is better worth their time? Can I motivate them *not* to click on the set, to involve themselves in something else?
- **Start them on another activity.** Take the time, set aside what you're doing, and get involved. Supervise the start of another activity: Choose a book together, lay out the ingredients for the next meal.

With these questions and suggestions, you can instill in your children the notion that "We don't watch TV, we watch TV *programs*." TV viewing should be a matter of choosing programs instead of mindlessly parking one's body in front of the TV set. Each viewing session should be time-bound; an agreement to watch should not be carte blanche to sit there for hours. Make it clear to your children that they should turn off the set after one or two programs.

The more your family's TV viewing becomes conscious, the greater your chances will be to turn it to more educational uses. Begin to think of television viewing as an intentional act. Intentional television can become intelligent television.

THE FAMILY TV DIET I:
YOU ARE WHAT
YOU WATCH

If you've read this far, you're now armed with statistics about the number of hours American kids spend watching television, an understanding of how overcommercialization of television leads to underserving children, and the effectiveness of TV as a teacher of violence and consumerism as well as of positive role models. What's a concerned parent to do? Hopefully, now you're ready to take action.

In this section, I present an approach to television that takes a middle path, that neither banishes TV from our homes as a worthless piece of furniture nor mindlessly continues its consumption for hours on end each day.

For most of us, eliminating TV from the household is not a practical alternative. When we need to clean the house, make dinner, or pay the bills, we can't devote our attention to our children—so television often steps in. And throwing out the TV also throws away some of the real benefits we and our children can enjoy from TV programming, if we use it wisely.

Intelligent use of television requires that we take control of the set, just as we control our children's bedtime, the toys they play with, and the food they eat.

This last analogy is the one I want to focus on: how we think about our children's diet provides a powerful model for how we can maximize the value of TV. In the two next chapters, I'll discuss how you can keep a TV diary and put your family on a TV Diet.

Watching TV Is Like Eating Dinner

Consider how you approach your family's diet. We should make the same informed choices about television shows as we do about food. Most parents don't let their children eat whatever they choose, whenever they choose. We understand that what our children put into their bodies affects their health, their energy level, and their mood. Most of us work to create a diet for our kids that is healthful and appealing.

In our lifetimes, our national consciousness about diet has changed. We've moved from the not-so-healthy idea of the Four Food Groups to adopting the new USDA's recommended pyramid of grains, vegetables, fruit, dairy, and meat.

Now we strive for a new "balanced meal" with less meat and fat and more grains, fruits, and vegetables. We shop smart; we read nutrition labels and try to minimize sugar, salt, and fat. And we try to avoid overeating from TV's Five Food Groups—McDonald's, Burger King, Wendy's, Taco Bell, and Pizza Hut.

At the same time, no one wants to be the Food Police. Food is still a source of pleasure in our family's lives. Even with more leafy greens and grains, there is room for our kids—and ourselves—to eat desserts, snacks, and treats.

Managing a family's diet and making food choices requires time, attention, and knowledge about nutritional content. It also takes a certain amount of resolve. Even with new knowledge about diet and nutrition, it is easy to eat the way our parents ate or to indulge our childhood favorites. I still look forward to my mother's pork-and-green onion dumplings, and I still like a fast-food hamburger and french fries. Eating habits start young and die hard.

So it is with television. For just about every concern we have about food, there's a parallel one for TV. We certainly spend a lot of time thinking about—and consuming—both. The two do converge, as audience research shows: We frequently eat while watching. If it's true that "you are what you eat," watch out! You may well become what you watch.

How Did Your Parents Use TV?

Let's look at some of the parallels, starting with how we were raised with TV. It's worth looking at how our parents used TV in order to make sense of our own use of the medium. As you consider your parents' home, and your own home, ask yourself these questions comparing how food and TV were used:

When you were growing up:
- What messages did your parents give you about TV?
- What kind of rules did they enforce around TV?
- Did they let you watch whatever you wanted? Or did they control the amount of viewing or types of shows you watched?

• Did your family have similar rules and attitudes about food? What were they?

Your own television and food habits:
• How much TV do you watch?
• When do you usually watch TV?
• Do you select TV shows, or do you just watch whatever's available?
• Do you watch more TV than you'd like to?
• Is the TV on in the house when no one is watching?
• How many TV sets are in your house? Where are they located—living room, den, bedrooms?
• Do family members watch together or by themselves? Which programs?
• Are you satisfied with your own food diet? Do you eat more than you'd like to?
• Have you ever gone on a diet or adjusted your diet?
• Would you consider doing the same for your TV watching?

Your children's television and food habits:
• Are there similarities and differences between how you deal with your children's diet and how you deal with their TV viewing?
• Does your home have rules about food? What, where, when, how much?
• Do you have rules about TV?
• Do you argue over meals, snacks, candy? How do you resolve those arguments?
• Do you argue over TV shows? How do you resolve those arguments?

• How does your own food diet compare with your children's diet? Do you treat your own diet differently from theirs? Do you also have different rules for your TV watching and theirs?

As the next chapters show, just as we can cut out or reduce the fat and junk food in our diets, we can—and must—reduce the hours we spend with junk TV.

"TV was a complete babysitter for me when I was growing up. I was a latchkey kid. It's still on at my mother's house 24 hours a day. I've broken that model. That's why I support the channels that I like, like public TV."

—*Gina, mother of a 15-month-old boy*

THE FAMILY TV DIET II: START WITH A CHART

Television watching is the default activity in most homes. The easiest thing to do at home is to flick on the TV set, surf the channels, settle on a bit of a sitcom here or a game show there, and before you know it, the evening is over. The TV set has become an electronic hearth, comforting to have on but not a source of much warmth. The greatest obstacle most families face in effectively using TV is in changing the amount of unthinking time we spend with television.

The first step in moving toward a reasonable TV diet is to take stock. In many diet plans, the first task is to write down everything you eat—from breakfast to the last cookie you had at midnight. Faced with an objective accounting of our diet, we are often amazed at how many of our calories come from fat and sugar. Fatty, sweet foods—against our better knowledge—are a habit. What kinds of TV shows make up the bulk of your TV menus?

Keeping a TV Diary

To break the habit of an unconscious TV diet, start by taking stock of how you and your children use TV. On a large sheet of paper or poster board, create a one-week calendar. Write the days of the week across the top, and the hours from wake-up to bedtime down the left side. Within each day, write the names of each family member.

Post the chart in a conspicuous place, such as on the refrigerator door. Every day, each person should keep track of what he watched and when. Or, one person could keep track of everyone's viewing by checking with each family member toward his or her bedtime.

Your TV Diary doesn't have to be neat and elegant. It's just a quick way to find out how much members of your family watch TV in a one week period. It doesn't matter if you start on a Monday or a Tuesday or in the dead of winter (though we do know that in colder climates, TV viewing goes up during the winter). The most important thing is to get started *now*.

You don't have to make the TV Diary exercise into a Major Family Project. Just let everyone know this is a little experiment you're going to try together. If you make a big deal out of it, you may become more self-conscious about your television viewing

> TV viewing is the number one activity for children in the hours between school and dinnertime. Nearly 80 percent of all kids report TV viewing as their usual activity then.
> —*1993 Yankelovich Youth Monitor survey of 1,200 children*

and suddenly watch less, or only watch certain shows. That step comes later. For now, keep quiet track of your family's normal viewing, and write it down in the diary.

Four Important Things to Do with Your TV Diary

• **Add it up.** Once you've charted out a week, add up the amount of time each family member has watched TV. Then gather the family around and take a look at who watched which programs. Before telling each family member their total viewing time, have them first estimate how many hours they spent watching TV that week. Are your children viewing at around the national average of four hours a day? More? Less?

• **Evaluate the programs you watched.** Briefly discuss the shows you've each watched. What do you remember about them? What did you like? What didn't you like? Would you watch the shows again? Were there shows that family members watched together? With older children, also ask if their viewing was planned or unplanned. If it was unplanned, what other activities could they have pursued?

• **Examine when the kids watch.** Look at the parts of the day in which your children watch television. Do they watch in the mornings before going to school or daycare? In the afternoons after coming home? In the early evening while dinner is being prepared? Evenings before bedtime? Saturday or Sunday morning? Discuss with your child her daily and weekly routine, and parts of the day that might be spent doing other things besides watching TV.

• **Evaluate your own time in front of the TV.** Look at your own viewing in a similar way. Look at the parts of the day in which you and your spouse watch TV. Which shows do you watch separately and which do you watch together? What is the total amount of time you spend watching, individually and together? Does your viewing time compare with the national average for adults, also about four hours a day? The Family TV Diet is about the whole family, about the time your children *and* you spend watching. Are there periods of your own TV watching that could be better spent in learning activities with your child?

Too Many TV Sets, Too Much Time

"I was born in 1959, so I was part of the first big TV generation. In 1965 we got our first color set—I remember the NBC peacock in color.

First, there were some good family times. We'd sit around *Flipper* together or the *Wizard of Oz* once a year. But then TV turned into something unhealthy for my family. It isolated us. We ended up with four TV sets in the house—two upstairs, two downstairs—so people would watch their own shows, alone. We'd watch at dinner, if my dad hadn't finished watching something he wanted.

I think my family missed out on some things. Instead of talking things out, we watched TV. Instead of dealing with relationships and problems, we watched TV."

—*Patrick, father of two sons, ages 4 and 5*

Walk the Walk and Talk the Talk

The goal is to cut back children's television viewing to about two hours a day *maximum*, as the PTA, the National Education

Association, the National Association for the Education of Young Children, and the American Academy of Pediatrics all agree. That means cutting the average viewing time for American children in half. But it is equally important for us as parents to alter our own viewing habits if necessary. Here's why:

- **You are your child's primary model.** If you watch more than 15 hours of television a week—upwards of 20, 30, or even 40 a week—you are probably modeling unconscious viewing for a good portion of that time.

- **You don't want to be a hypocrite.** If you require your children to cut back on their TV viewing, but they see you watching for hours at a time, they can rightfully question the fairness of your edict. They'll learn that it's okay for parents to say one thing but do another. Instead of moving toward a joint effort to regulate TV in your home, your efforts could backfire and lead to more conflict around TV viewing.

- **Your time is their time.** This may be the most important point of all. The less time you spend watching *Roseanne* or football, the more time you have for your children—and the more time you have to share an activity with them.

These hours are the real "prime time" where you can serve as an educator for your child. These are the hours your children will remember most when they grow up, the times when you showed them how to make a bird feeder, or took them to a museum, or coached their soccer team.

When you look at your TV Diary, pay attention to the hours when both you and your child are watching TV. Are you watching different programs in separate rooms? Toddlers often engage in "parallel play," where they play alongside each other, but not with each other, because they don't yet have the language and social skills to engage in playful interaction.

You and your child might be engaging in "parallel viewing," where you both have the time to do something together and have chosen to do the same thing—only separately. These hours are prime candidates for "family learning hours" that you can spend together.

THE FAMILY TV DIET III:
A DIET FOR
THE SMALL SCREEN

The comparisons between how we use food and how we use TV are telling. As a nation, the disturbing truth is we eat too much and we watch too much. The problem is becoming acute among our children. According to the Amateur Athletic Union (AAU), from 1980 to 1989, the average weight of American girls, ages 12 and 13, increased by more than nine pounds. Boys aged 14 to 17 got five pounds heavier. Only 32 percent of our children ages six to 17 can pass the AAU's physical-fitness test. One-third of boys and 50 percent of girls cannot run a mile in less than 10 minutes. American kids are among the most obese and unfit in the world.

Placing your family on a TV Diet is mainly intended to help your children cut down on empty TV calories and exercise their intellectual muscles. But by freeing up time away from TV, a TV Diet can also make more time available for physical fitness.

What is a Family TV Diet? It's not a set of prescribed TV shows for you to consume, with a verified nutritional content. It doesn't come packaged with menus and powders for you to mix with water. It's a plan for using TV that you create with your partner and with your child. It's an approach to TV that your family can personalize, keeping three basic principles in mind.

> American schoolchildren watch an average of 4 hours of TV a day, 28 a week, 1,400 a year, and close to 18,000 by the time they graduate from high school.

Principle #1: Bringing Consumption Under Control: Two Hours Maximum a Day

If you're like the average American family, chances are you're watching too much TV. The national average is around four hours a day, which means that many kids are watching five, seven, or even more hours a day! For most kids, the TV Diet should begin by reducing their total consumption of TV calories. Four hours a day is simply too much time taken away from other worthwhile activities, hobbies, and interests.

In most families, going on a TV Diet will mean cutting your total viewing time by about half, to average about two hours a day or 14 to 15 total hours per week. For some kids, this will mean cutting back even more. The TV Diary in the previous chapter will help you get started by examining where your family can cut back.

The TV–Obesity Connection

Does TV make you fat? Some studies report a connection between overweight American kids and adults and the hours they watch TV.

Tufts University pediatrician Dr. William Dietz Jr. and Dr. Steven Gortmaker of the Harvard School of Public Health studied the health and viewing habits of 1,500 American children. Their findings confirmed the obvious: Too much TV leaves little time for physical activity. With each hour of TV that a child views daily, his risk for obesity increases. Ten percent of adolescents who watched less than one hour of television per day were obese. But among those who watched five hours a day or more, 20 percent were obese.

"I think parents must understand that TV constitutes a major health problem for children," says Dietz. "Time in front of the TV is time that is taken away from other activities, especially more participatory activities."

Other research with adult men and women has demonstrated similar direct links between body weight and hours of TV viewing: A 1991 study of 6,000 men found that those who watched more than three hours of television daily were twice as likely to be obese as those who watched less than an hour.

For most families, the most difficult part of the Family TV Diet may be changing habits. Changing the amount of time your child spends watching TV can become a source of conflict, between you, your partner, and your child, just as many families already experience conflicts over who watches what, and when.

In our family, Ruth has been better at setting up rules for Maggie and following through on them. Often, I've been the one to let her have that extra piece of candy or stay up a half-hour later. Over the years, how Ruth and I approach limit-setting has become an obvious issue for us to work on together.

We are getting better at it. For instance, we recently set a rule that Maggie can watch one hour of TV or a video at 7 pm, after dinner and before going to bed. In the beginning, Maggie would attempt to bargain with me to allow her to start watching earlier or to watch an extra show. But Ruth and I discussed this rule and have put up a united front.

From our experiences with setting limits around TV, we have learned two important things. One: Clarity about TV rules is important. In order for the rules to work, this clarity must be shared among all family members. Two: Children respond once they know the limits. With TV, as in other areas of their lives, children appreciate having clear expectations.

Some critics of TV have said we must boycott television and throw away our sets. I believe this extreme reaction does away with the good that TV can do, as well as the bad. This extreme solution may work temporarily, but in the long run, we often revert back to our old habits. The "crash diet" scenario is also impractical for many modern families.

I do suggest, however, that families experiment with modifying their TV habits to meet their own needs and schedules. For some families, a TV Turn-Off Week (or Month) may be a good idea. Others may want to reduce TV viewing gradually by a few hours each week. There are even gadgets that enable you to lock out your TV set during programming that you deem off-limits to your children, or issue "credit cards" to family members, redeemable for viewing hours.

You might also find some help from an unlikely source—a children's book. One of the popular Berenstain Bear books is titled *Too Much TV*. At Mama Bear's suggestion, the Bear Family takes a break from TV for a week. In those hours, Brother and Sister Bear ride bikes, play with puzzles, and take time to look at the stars. The family member who has the most difficulty, however, is Papa Bear, who has trouble giving up his sports and game shows. If you read this story with your child, you might see that this family of bears is more like your own than you think.

Principle #2: Preparing a Balanced TV Meal

Think about selecting TV shows the way you choose food in the supermarket. To prepare a balanced TV meal, make intentional choices about the TV your child watches.

By "shopping" for your child's TV shows, you set out to bring certain shows into your home. You make TV viewing a set of intentional acts, instead of just allowing "whatever's on." Shopping also empowers you to evaluate programs and to choose those with "higher nutritional content" over those that are junk.

For "main courses," select programs that have some educational or informational value. These "dishes" should be worthwhile programs that can lead to other areas of knowledge and activity and link up with some other domain of your child's life, such as school subjects, homework, hobbies, or summer activities. Just as snacks and dessert are fine in moderation, you can also allow some programs for purely entertainment purposes.

Some parents might be somewhat dubious—will kids really like "nutritious TV"? In our research on *3-2-1 Contact* at the Children's Television Workshop, I was struck by the different "appetites" children have related to television viewing. The same children who loved action/adventure shows, such as *The $6 Million Man*, also expressed a real curiosity and yearning to learn about science. Just as their bodies prefer varied and balanced meals, children will also take to programs that feed their minds.

The Family TV Diet requires that you become knowledgeable consumers of children's TV. As you're considering what shows to include in your Family TV Diet, exercise the same type of thinking as when you're walking down the supermarket aisle and putting items in the cart. Check the labels. Consider the ingredients in the shows you would like your child to watch, their main characters and messages.

This is where you need to do a little homework to learn more about the shows that are available. In this sense, children's television needs to become parents' television as well. Parents who are well informed about an educational program's goals and subject matter, whether geography or reading, will be in the best position to reinforce them.

The best way to learn about what your children are watching is to watch a few shows from a series with them. By "co-viewing" with your children, you send a message that you value those programs, and you'll be better able to discuss their content and connect them with follow-up activities.

Unfortunately, it's not that easy to find out about quality children's shows, when they're broadcast, and what their goals are. Newspaper TV listings can be fairly cryptic, especially when it comes to children's and educational shows. *TV Guide* is more helpful by giving fuller program descriptions.

Each spring and fall, *TV Guide* devotes an entire issue to the best children's programming, including experts' favorites. Keep your eyes open for recommendations in newspapers and parents' magazines. Member guides published by your local PBS station may also describe current and new children's shows and specials. See the list at the end of this chapter for some recommended children's shows.

> "A program is something your child will spend time with. So ask yourself, Do I want my child to hang out with this person and this program?"
>
> —*Patrick, father of two sons, ages 4 and 5*

Principle #3: Don't Just Sit There After Eating

If you and your child select quality shows as the main course, this step of the TV Diet can really start to pay educational dividends for your child. Conventional wisdom says digestion is aided by staying active after a meal. The worst thing to do is go to sleep after eating. Likewise, you shouldn't just sit around after a TV program. Educational shows can tie in naturally with follow-up activities that your child can do or that you can do together after the set is turned off.

In Part IV, I give examples of programs that you can connect with book reading, museum visits, board games, and other family activities. View these as suggestions, or "sample recipes," that can be adjusted to your own taste and preferences. Then come up with your own!

Create a Democracy, Not a Dictatorship

When it comes to children's TV, many of us take a laissez-faire, hands-off approach. Can you think of another sphere of children's life where we habitually let strangers decide what they will hear, see, or do? Yet many parents do precisely that by allowing children to watch whatever they want, whenever they want. TV watching should be no different from any other activity. Exercise your parental prerogative.

This does not mean you should act by fiat and dictate what is on the dial. As your child enters the preschool years, I encourage you to involve her in these decisions, just as she voices her opinions about what she likes to eat.

If your Family TV Diet evolves out of shared discussion and negotiation, your child will feel more committed to a viewing plan. The TV Diet should give her a stake in her own TV viewing and the understanding that TV viewing is an activity she can control, rather than the other way around.

Act authoritatively and firmly, involving your children in developing the rules they are to live by. Though your Family TV Diet should be based on parental authority and leadership, it should also be a participatory form of government.

Give your children a vote and a voice. Help them develop a healthy sense of responsibility for their actions and decisions. Most importantly, use the TV Diet as an occasion to discuss what you're watching, what you're getting from it, and why.

The Best Kids' Shows

Hall of Fame for Preschool Shows
Sesame Street (PBS)
Mister Rogers' Neighborhood (PBS)
Shining Time Station (PBS)

10 Best Preschool Shows
1. *Bobby's World* (Fox)
2. *Bookmice* (Learning Channel)
3. *The Busy World of Richard Scarry* (Showtime)
4. *Eureeka's Castle* (Nickelodeon)
5. *Gerbert* (local public TV)
6. *Jim Henson's The Secret Life of Toys* (Disney Channel)
7. *Lamb Chop's Play-Along* (PBS)
8. *Madeline* (Family Channel)
9. *Twinkle, the Dream Being* (syndicated)
10. *The World of Peter Rabbit and Friends* (The Family Channel)

Hall of Fame for School-Age Shows
ABC After-School Specials
CBS Schoolbreak Specials
Reading Rainbow (PBS)

Top 10 School-Age Shows
1. *Are You Afraid of the Dark?* (Nickelodeon)
2. *Beakman's World* (CBS)
3. *Bill Nye, the Science Guy* (Disney Channel; PBS)
4. *Clarissa Explains It All* (Nickelodeon)
5. *Cro* (ABC)
6. *Ghostwriter* (PBS)
7. *Name Your Adventure* (NBC)

8. *Nick News* (Nickelodeon)
9. *Roundhouse* (Nickelodeon)
10. *Steven Spielberg Presents Animaniacs* (Fox)
—TV Guide, *March 12, 1994*

But most American children, especially six- to 11-year-olds, are watching other commercial shows.

Top 10 Weekend Daytime Programs with Children, 2-11
1. *X-Men* (Fox)
2. *Tiny Toons* (Fox)
3. *Bobby's World* (Fox)
4. *EEK the Cat* (Fox)
5. *Taz-mania* (Fox)
6. *Terrible Thunderlizards* (Fox)
7. *Super Dave Special* (Fox)
8. *Garfield and Friends* (CBS)
9. *Mighty Morphin Power Rangers* (Fox)
10. *Teenage Mutant Ninja Turtles* (CBS)

Top 10 Evening Programs with Children, 2–11
1. *Edith Ann* (ABC)
2. *Critic* (ABC)
3. *Step by Step* (ABC)
4. *Full House* (ABC)
5. *Boy Meets World* (ABC)
6. *Home Improvement* (ABC)
7. *Family Matters* (ABC)
8. *The Simpsons* (Fox)
9. *America's Funniest Home Videos* (ABC)
10. *Hangin' with Mr. Cooper* (ABC)

—Nielsen Television Index, *January 1994*

THE VCR: THE PRINTING PRESS IN YOUR LIVING ROOM

Of recent great inventions that have changed our lives, the VCR ranks right up there with the answering machine, the personal computer, and the microwave. It is hard to imagine life in our times without them.

Among American families, the VCR is nearly universal, enabling us to take greater control over when and what we watch on television. By taping programs with the VCR, we are liberated from the broadcasters' schedules and can create our own. Young parents who go to bed by 10 pm tell me that *The Late Show with David Letterman* actually goes well with cornflakes in the morning.

Of course, our viewing choices have also multiplied—not only do we have more channels than ever before, but we have even greater selections at neighborhood video rental stores. Today it is easier than ever to find programs that match our personal interests, from science to classic movies to how-to shows.

From a Mass Medium to a Personal One

With the advent of the VCR, we entered the era of personal television. In the days when ABC, CBS, and NBC ruled, TV was called a "mass medium," because it reached so many Americans. As we move from 10 broadcast channels to 50 cable channels to upwards of 100 channels, TV is being "demassified" into numerous channels that appeal to smaller, specialized niche audiences. Unfortunately, there is still no single educational channel that your children can turn to for quality programming whenever they want to watch.

The VCR can be a real ally in your efforts to create a personalized channel and a healthy TV Diet. It allows you to choose beyond what broadcasters are serving up.

Think of your VCR as a video printing press in your own home. It enables you to select quality children's shows and create a home video library that can be used as an alternative to broadcast channels. You can unchain your children and yourselves from the tyranny of TV schedules.

Here are some simple reminders of how to discover and use the rich video resources already available simply by using the Record and Play buttons on your VCR:

> 78 percent of American homes have a VCR.

- **Invest in a VCR that is easy to program.** Ten years ago, it was true that "99 percent of the VCRs in this country are blinking 12:00." Today, newer VCRs, with on-screen programming, guide you to use the remote control to set the time and channel

Your VCR: A Video Crockpot

A teacher once told me the lengths to which she went to record educational programs. Many PBS stations, including KQED, broadcast instructional TV shows for teachers to videotape. In the predawn hours, these high-quality programs are often broadcast in back-to-back segments, so that teachers and parents can videotape an entire series.

A two-hour broadcast of a high school French program would not attract much of a home audience during the day. But at 3 am, when the home audience is minimal, teachers and parents can put those overnight hours to good use with a VCR to accumulate a home or school video library.

This teacher wanted desperately to record the overnight "block broadcast" of shows for her school, but couldn't figure out how to set her VCR timer to record from 2 to 4 am. I asked her how she recorded the shows.

"Well," she said, "before I go to bed, I put in a blank tape and set the VCR to your channel. I then set my alarm clock to 2 am. It wakes me up, I race over to the VCR, press Record, and then go back to sleep. When I wake up, my videos are all ready. It's like a Video Crockpot!"

you wish to record. The VCR Plus remote control device has also simplified the task of setting your VCR.

- **Pay attention to local listings.** Keep track of what's on and when. Then tape some of the excellent children's specials broadcast during the holidays or heritage months, such as Black History Month in February or Hispanic Heritage Month in September.

- **Create a video library of kids' favorites.** Make it a point to tape programs from educational series such as *Sesame Street,*

Ghostwriter, or *Reading Rainbow.* A video library with five or 10 shows from several series can be an ongoing educational resource in your home.

Many children enjoy and learn from repeated viewings of favorite programs, just as they do from hearing the same bedtime story over and over. The Russians say *Povtorenia mat uchenia,* which translates to "Repetition is the mother of learning."

- **Shop around for bargains.** Children's videos seem to be sold everywhere now, from video and toy stores to supermarkets. I once paid $5 for a *Charlie Brown* video during a gas station promotion. You can also buy children's movies on videocassette shortly after they play in movie houses, like Disney's *Beauty and the Beast* and *Peter Pan.* While these cassettes often cost $20 or more, we have bought a few and shared them with families who, in turn, let us borrow theirs.

- **Organize your home video library near the TV and VCR.** Label the videos clearly, with the title of the series, the title of each individual program, and the length of the show. That way, you and your child will know how long each program is and how much of it he'll watch at one sitting.

- **Turn to your video library before you turn on the TV.** When your child says he wants to watch TV, ask him to consider whether there is a show he would like to watch on cassette. Teach him to consider the home video library as an alternative source of programming.

- **Cruise the children's section of your local video store.** Many families rent videos for their kids to watch on Friday and Saturday nights. It's cheaper than going to the movies, and the selection is much greater. But I urge you not to let your child simply go to the children's section and choose whatever he wants. Just because a video is for children doesn't mean it's *good* for children.

- **Help your children make better choices.** Try to direct them to higher quality movies and programs. Inspiring stories such as *Anne of Green Gables* (seen on PBS and cable) and *The Secret Garden* are better choices for a school-age child than the hit movie of the day, be it *Dennis the Menace* or *Monkey Trouble*.

Look for other movies or programs featuring young people who, faced with difficult situations, act with courage and integrity. These characters can serve as role models for your children.

- **Talk about your video choices.** Does the movie you're renting have a message or a character you'd like your child to know about? Reinforce those messages and talk with your child about them, using people and situations from your own lives.

Also consider whether there's a companion book your child can read. *Anne of Green Gables* is perfect for children who can read at around the sixth-grade level. Though this excellent series of videos and books tends to be favored more by girls than boys, it's as important for boys as for girls to see TV shows with young girls who are smart, independent, and resourceful.

Children's videos are big business. In 1992, Americans bought 265 million videos, spending about $52 per household. Children's videos accounted for 36 percent of total unit sales, or about $1.36 billion, the second highest category after feature films (45 percent). In 1993, 16 of the top 20 videos sold in video stores were bought by families with children, including *Aladdin*, *The Little Mermaid*, and *Barney*.

PART IV

Weaving a Web

of Learning for

Your Child

TV AS A SPRINGBOARD
FOR EDUCATIONAL
EXPERIENCES

Now that you're working on consuming a healthier TV Diet and you've got your VCR revved up, it's time to convert calories from programming that's viewed to those from programming that is used. This section is about how parents can introduce subjects such as reading, math, and science to our children in a more modern way—via educational TV—and how we can relate those TV shows to other learning experiences in and out of the classroom.

Once your child is watching TV programs with an educational content, you can supplement TV viewing with a host of related interests, activities, and discussions. Television programs from *Sesame Street* to *National Geographic Specials* can carry your child from the preschool years through adolescence, serving as springboards into other learning activities.

Think of it as weaving a web of learning activities with your child that includes TV shows, books, experiments, drawings, writings, audios, videos, computers, and trips to the public library, science center, children's museum, nature preserve, factory, or just the park nearby. TV can become part of the educational fabric in your home and lead you to resources in your community. By guiding your child toward these experiences and working with him to absorb their educational value, you can act as a powerful educator.

> "Television sparks curiosity and opens up distant worlds to children. Through its magic, youngsters can travel to the moon or the bottom of the sea. They can visit medieval castles, take river trips, or explore imaginary lands....With selective viewing, television can richly contribute to school readiness."
> —*Dr. Ernest Boyer, President, Carnegie Foundation for the Advancement of Teaching and former US Commissioner of Education*

Weaving a Learning Web

Once you begin paying attention to what interests your child, you'll see that many other related opportunities present themselves. Here is a fictional scenario written by media researcher Dr. Valerie Crane describing how a parent and child can weave a web of learning around a particular subject, in this case, whales:

Early in September, eight-year-old Cindy rises and gets ready for school. While waiting for her mother, she goes into the living room and turns on the TV, which shows the wonders of the migration of whales. Cindy is intrigued with the size and power of the whales, and she reflects on this as she heads for school.

Months later Cindy recalls this moment when her teacher assigns the class to small groups which sort and classify the different foods that whales eat. As part of this unit, her assignment is to write an ecology essay on the food chain.

Over the Christmas holidays, her uncle spends some time with her and shares a map on the migration patterns of whales. Later that spring, Cindy's mother sees a story on the local news about some beached whales about a half-hour from where they live. She calls Cindy in to watch, and they talk about how whales are the biggest mammals and how they would all die if it weren't for the littlest microscopic animals in the sea that they eat.

Cindy writes to the local television station to find out more. The station sends her a brochure on whales, explaining the phenomenon. The brochure suggests a visit to the aquarium to look at a new exhibit which shows a baby dolphin being born. She asks her mother if they can visit the aquarium sometime. Cindy's mother remembers her request several months later when they are planning activities for a rainy day during the summer. Cindy notices how the exhibit explains how big fish eat smaller fish—something she had written about in her ecology paper for school.

Learning—and Unlearning—Together

To begin acting as an educator for your child, you may first need to unlearn some things you've been taught. Chances are, the way you were taught in school isn't the way you would like to teach and interact with your children. Remember the importance of getting the right answer? Getting it fast? Doing your own work? No talking! Do you hear the voice of your fourth-grade teacher?

Fortunately, we've arrived at a new view of what education is about and what children can learn. Children are wired to learn.

The curriculum has finally caught up with the kids. You can do a science experiment with your five-year-old. You can begin to introduce her to the cultures and geography of the world. You can help your child learn in ways that are more exciting for her and more rewarding for you. You may learn some new things, too.

Hopefully, your child is receiving these messages in her classroom or childcare setting. When parents and teachers work together, reinforcing each other's philosophies, a powerful synergy is established between the home and the school. This is when children make the most of their time spent in both places and can make tremendous strides in their learning.

Discovering New Learning Resources

While children's television and video have a long way to go in fulfilling their promises, there is an adequate choice of programs parents can use to support their children's learning, on broadcast and cable channels. One of the chief obstacles for parents is obtaining information about what's available, when it's available, and what related materials are available, such as books or activity guides. There's no real reason why an adult would have occasion to tune into children's shows in advance of being a parent.

In talks with parents, I am constantly surprised by how little information parents have about children's TV programming. Everyone seems familiar with *Sesame Street* and *Barney*, but many have not heard of *Square One TV*, *Ghostwriter*, or *I'll Fly Away*.

While public television has many quality shows for children, it has relatively few funds to promote them directly to parents, teachers, and childcare providers. Currently, several efforts in public television are in progress, such as a new national "Ready to Learn" project, to let people know about its resources, which often include viewer guides, book lists, and workshops for parents and educators. Cable channels, such as Nickelodeon, and commercial networks are also making efforts to better inform the public about quality children's shows.

Consult the Resource Guide for further organizations, viewer guides, and other materials to help you become a more informed consumer of children's TV. Take the time to find out what's available both locally and nationally.

In the following chapters, you'll find some specific ideas about shows that you and your child can weave into a web of learning. These ideas are only intended as examples: Use your own creativity and background, as well as your child's interests, in deciding what topics to pursue. Once you become familiar with educational programs, you will see many connections between them and other resources in your home, school, and community.

HOW TO TALK SO KIDS WILL LEARN: FOSTERING AN EDUCATIONAL DIALOGUE

Years ago, a popular parenting book, called *How to Talk So Kids Will Listen and Listen So Kids Will Talk,* made the rounds. There should be a companion book, on how to talk to children in a way that inspires and promotes their learning.

You can engage your children in an ongoing educational dialogue. Many parents, when confronted with advice from experts to "talk to your kids," are puzzled by what that means. What is an "educational dialogue"? What do we talk about? How?

Maggie Comer, mother of the distinguished educator Dr. James Comer, understood the importance of creating an educational dialogue with her children (see page 128). As she and her kids sat on the bus, she would point out the window to things of interest or help them interpret the ads posted on the bus. She seized every opportunity, even the most mundane, to teach her children about the world.

Creating an educational dialogue is really not very hard. All it takes is a recognition that you are your child's first teacher and a commitment to engaging your children in a process of continuous questioning, discussing, and explaining. Don't worry, you don't have to know all the answers. As Benjamin Spock counsels new parents, "You know more than you think you do." Most importantly, you know how to help your children find out what they need to know.

Explaining the World—at a Child's Height

A parent can serve as an "explainer" of the world to your child. You don't have to be an expert, but you have to be interested in guiding the process. At the Exploratorium in San Francisco, a world-renowned science center, young teens are trained to serve as "explainers" of exhibits to children and adults. The teens are not experts, but they know enough to advance a child's or an adult's understanding another level or two. They encourage visitors to look at an exhibit, ask questions, and start a brief discussion. They communicate that the scientific phenomena are intriguing and worth thinking about, and that learning about them can be enjoyable and even hip.

With preschoolers, it's easy to explain the world just by pointing out and talking about the everyday things you see on a walk, a drive, or at the supermarket. As your kids get older, you can become more of a coach as you encourage their interests and lead them to find resources.

Maggie's American Dream

Any committed parent can sustain an educational dialogue with his or her child. One of the best descriptions of how it's done comes from an oral history told by Maggie Comer to her son, Dr. James Comer, a nationally renowned child psychiatrist and educator at the Yale Medical School. The book is titled, *Maggie's American Dream: The Life and Times of a Black Family.*

James Comer and his four siblings didn't come from a privileged background. Their father worked in the steel plants of Gary, Indiana, and his mother cleaned houses. Yet, this hard-working couple placed education as the highest priority for their children—and the five Comer children went on to earn 13 college and advanced degrees. Hugh and Maggie Comer believed in their children's talents and made a commitment to nurturing them, as Maggie Comer explains:

> I believe in talking with children, taking time with them, taking them to places of interest, doing things together. But everybody don't see it that way....Parents get on a bus and flop down and just sit and stare. But when kids are small, you can teach them a lot. You can read these different advertisements on the ceiling and point out different things....Just be talking—answering questions, making them think about things....
>
> Children see this thing and that thing and don't understand it. They ask Mom or Dad, "Why is this thing over here?" or "Why is this man standing here?" You explain to the child and they want to learn more.

Television programs, like bus ads, can provide the basis for these ongoing conversations. But I couldn't have said it better than Maggie Comer.

Curiosity and Other Tools

Have a good dictionary, atlas, and encyclopedia handy, and teach your kids to consult them, as well as teachers, family members, and your local library, for more information. When your child learns that she can find answers on her own, she's well on her way to the most important outcome of this ongoing dialogue: She's becoming an independent learner.

There is a certain art to explaining. Good teachers and tour guides do it all the time. They explain things at the level of their learners, but also present and define new words and concepts. They encourage questions as a way of tailoring the presentation and checking for comprehension. They don't over-explain.

Good "explainers" are passionate about their subjects. As a parent, you have enormous power to convey to your child the importance you place on learning and the passion you feel about your favorite subjects. These are values parents communicate to their children when they explain that the world is full of interesting people, places, and ideas, and that learning about them can be a source of lifelong enjoyment.

HOW TO READ
A VIDEO

If you peruse the parenting section of any bookstore, you'll notice several books on how to read books to children. I like one by Paul Copperman titled *Taking Books to Heart: How to Develop a Love of Reading in Your Child* (even if he has been misled by too many myths about TV). He demonstrates how parents can adopt a style of reading to their children that is much more than just reading text.

His suggestions on reading a book to children apply to "reading a video," too. For example, Copperman and others suggest that parents supply a running commentary on the text and illustrations, check your child's understanding of the vocabulary, and elaborate on the story based on your or your child's experiences.

To illustrate his technique, Copperman turns to that wonderful story by Maurice Sendak, *Where the Wild Things Are*, where young Max journeys to the Land of the Wild Things.

130

Here are Copperman's suggestions on how parents can elaborate on the text and illustrations:

> ...you might say something like this: "Ah! See? Here's Max, telling the Wild Things to 'BE STILL!' See how they listen to him? Immediately they sit down. Now he's going to stare into their eyes."... You can add layers of appreciation to the illustration. You might point out how the Wild Things now seem to be in fear of Max, or that Max doesn't appear as happy with them as he was earlier.... You might ask [your child] what a particular Wild Thing is thinking at this point, or what Max is thinking....When you engage in dialogue like this, you provide your child with a model of comprehension, a demonstration of how to think while reading.

Most importantly, Copperman urges parents to make book reading fun by gently encouraging and modeling how to look at a story and put together its pieces instead of insistently correcting their children's reading.

Teachable Moments on Pages and on Screens

Educational television can provide the same raw material for thinking, reflection, and enjoyment. Unfortunately, we don't typically think of discussing and analyzing TV in this way. But just as you can read a book with your child, you can apply the same techniques to video, commenting on the images and tying the dialogue or narration to them. Together you can summarize, clarify, and predict what will happen next. You and your child can "read a video."

In our instructional TV workshops at KQED, we've found that expert teachers use video in this way in their classrooms. They

Are Lectures Better Live or
When They're Memorex?

One unusual study shows the benefits of teachers and students "reading videos" together. Dr. James Gibbons, former dean and professor of engineering at Stanford, compared a group of engineering graduate students who took a course by video with the group of students who took the course in the traditional fashion by attending lectures on campus. Both groups of students followed the same course syllabus and took the same exams. On the final exam, the group who experienced the lectures on video outperformed the students who heard it live.

How could this happen? The students in the first group "read" and analyzed the videotaped lectures with a tutor. As they watched the videotaped lectures, they paused the tape to ask questions or have brief discussions. Gibbons and his colleagues write that this tutored videotape instruction "is based on the common-sense notion that students can learn more from a lecture if they are free to interrupt it at places where they need more discussion or explanation of a point or concept. Experience over the past three years shows that students learn best when the videotaped lectures are stopped frequently, for example, every five to 10 minutes, for periods of three to five minutes."

The "teachable moment"—that moment when a student has formulated a question and is ready for an answer—tends to get lost in a large lecture hall. It's helpful to have "the instant replay" on video and a supportive tutor to talk to nearby. When it comes to using educational videos with children, parents can play the crucial role of tutor.

use the pause button on the VCR to allow time for thinking and discussion.

Instead of turning on a video and sitting in the back grading papers, these teachers remain at the front of the class or stroll the aisles with a remote control. They frequently interrupt the program to stimulate classroom discussion, calling out questions, checking students' understanding, and interacting with them in a spirited dialogue about what they're seeing. The VCR enables the teachers to use the video materials more interactively. Likewise, the teachers are helping the students turn the viewing experience into an active thinking process.

A colleague, Bill Marsh, and I call this viewing style "actively viewed video." As a parent, you can do it, too. Here are some basic ingredients for a successful "co-viewing" experience:

- **Identify a video you want to read with your child.** This works best if you have the program on videocassette, either recorded or rented. But it can also work if you watch a broadcast show together.

- **Encourage your child to ask questions.** When you watch together, ask her to ask you to explain anything she doesn't understand.

- **Comment on the show.** Look for opportunities to explain the story, the characters, and the content. Ask your child to predict what's going to happen next.

- **Connect your comments to your child's experiences.** Think about what your child will find familiar.

- **Talk about what you've seen.** When the video is over, take the time to discuss it.

- **Make it fun.** Tell your child you've enjoyed sharing this activity with her.
- **Plan to watch other programs together.** Look for videos or programs on the same topic, or other interesting topics you'd like to watch together.

By using videos in this way, you are helping your child learn to think, reflect, acquire new knowledge, and assimilate ideas. You're training her to think critically. And, most importantly, you're helping her enjoy doing it.

GATHER 'ROUND THE ELECTRONIC HEARTH: CREATING FAMILY EVENTS AROUND TV

Watching television together can be an important shared experience between parents and children. You'll find that educational shows often fill in gaps in your own experience and learning. For instance, I enjoy watching segments on how things are made, such as a trip to a crayon factory on *Mister Rogers' Neighborhood*, or how a master craftsman makes a violin, on *Reading Rainbow*.

Watching together can strengthen the family bond and create opportunities to link programs with other educational activities. *Sesame Street* research also points out that children who are encouraged to watch by their parents and who "co-view" with them show the greatest learning gains.

You can gather the family around many high-quality programs and practice "reading" them together. Many families also make a special event out of watching a new show or TV special together.

This past winter, Maggie, Ruth, and I joined many millions of people around the world in watching the 1994 Winter Olympics from Norway. It was the first Olympics that Maggie, now seven, took an interest in. We cheered for Bonnie Blair and Dan Jansen and felt Nancy Kerrigan really did deserve that gold medal.

We also learned more about the people and cultures of Norway, such as the Samis, the indigenous Scandinavians who performed in the opening ceremonies. Previously, Maggie and I had read a children's book, *Far North: Vanishing Cultures,* profiling the Sami people.

When we saw the Samis performing traditional dances in the Olympics, we reread the book. It was an example of the serendipitous connections to be found between television and other educational activities.

> "Now that the boys are older, we're watching more science shows. It's great that they can see different situations and learn from them. On *Newton's Apple* they just learned how a dollar bill changer can take their money and know that it is a dollar, not a piece of paper. And on *Sesame Street,* they see so much, like someone who's blind or in a wheelchair, and they talk about it. TV can give them more experiences, more insight from outside their world."
> —*Cynthia, mother of two boys ages 5 and 6*

Help Your Child "View Up"

One way in which you can help your child "read a video" and create a family event around a program is to pick a show that challenges all of you. Younger children want to do what "bigger kids" get to do. Just as younger siblings want to dress and act like their older brothers and sisters, they often want to watch the same TV shows. They like to "view up." (However, it's hard to get an older child to watch something intended for younger kids.)

You can help introduce your children to shows for the next age group. For instance, with five- and six-year-olds, try watching *Ghostwriter* or *Square One TV* together. Though these programs are aimed at the next older age group, younger kids can get a lot from them, with a little help from Mom or Dad.

In the summer of 1991, *Child* magazine surveyed its subscribers on how they use television.
- 71 percent said they were most troubled by TV violence.
- 65 percent have a rule relating to prohibiting certain programs.
- 65 percent said children benefit from TV viewing by learning reading and language skills.
- 63 percent said TV benefited children's science and nature learning.
- 39 percent have a rule restricting viewing time.

Prime Learning on Prime Time

I have been impressed at how early some parents introduce their children to prime-time educational shows produced for adults, such as *National Geographic Special* programs, *NOVA*, or biographical documentaries, such as the *American Experience* program on Malcolm X. By the time your child is eight or nine years old, you might consider introducing him to a program that you find especially interesting. Ideally, you can link this shared viewing to a school assignment in geography, science, or history.

You might plan to watch a broadcast together, or, better yet, record the program on your VCR. As you watch, practice "reading the video," interpreting the visuals and audio track, explaining unfamiliar vocabulary, or helping place locations or historical events in context. Even if your child only watches half of an hour-long program, she will have learned some key information that she can return to later. And you will have signified your interest in that topic to her.

My wife and I watched a *National Geographic Special* with Maggie in this way. Last year, as we traveled through Kruger National Park in South Africa, we saw lions, elephants, giraffes, rhinoceroses, and other large game, up close and personal, from the safety of our rental car. Shortly after we returned home, public TV aired *Reflections on Elephants*, filmed in Botswana. This captivating look at wild elephants follows an elephant herd, as they adopt an abandoned male calf, an unusual behavior.

Though the program used language Maggie did not understand, the visual images were gripping. We explained that Botswana was a country next to South Africa and commented on how the scenes from the African bush looked very much like where we had been.

Maggie asked about words she heard, such as "What's a matriarch?" and "What does 'abandoned' mean?" She saw how the elephant herd adopted the baby elephant. "They figured the baby was going to slow them down," she commented, noting what had been said by the narrator. "At least he has someone to go with." She learned that lions hunt elephants and that the dirt and sand elephants eat contain important minerals and sodium. She laughed when a baby elephant had its first bowel movement and fell in a patch of mud.

She paid attention for the first 40 minutes of the hour-long show, but she did have a vivid visual experience that connected and reinforced with other things she had seen and heard in person on our trip. This was the kind of program we might watch or record when it is rebroadcast.

We'll keep an eye out for stories about elephants and other African animals. Some day, she'll have a pool of knowledge to use in researching and writing a school assignment. Part of our family's web of learning now involves the wildlife and people of this part of Africa we've visited.

"My kids wanted to watch the Malcolm X documentary. They really got into it and asked a lot of questions. Our 14-year-old, Nikia, read his autobiography three years ago. We've purchased some videos about him. I didn't discover Malcolm X until I was in college. Now, they learn about him in high school."
—Kevin, father of a son and two daughters, ages 4, 9, and 14

THE SPECIAL LANGUAGE OF MISTER ROGERS

I confess that, until I was a parent and observed my daughter watching *Mister Rogers' Neighborhood*, I didn't fully appreciate the magic of Fred Rogers.

A few years ago, I was at a meeting with Bill Isler, vice president of Family Communications, Inc., the *Mister Rogers' Neighborhood* production company. I mentioned that my daughter was about to turn five. Bill said, "That's great! Let me have Fred send her a birthday card." Sure enough, a few days later, a card arrived for Maggie, signed by Mister Rogers.

When I gave the card to Maggie, I was interested in her reaction. She smiled broadly and said, "How did he know it was my birthday?" I explained and asked her why she liked Mister Rogers. She looked at me and said simply, "Because there's a special language for talking to children, and Mister Rogers knows the special language."

Bringing the Neighborhood to
Childcare Providers

In 1990, Fred Rogers began taking his message to the childcare community. Through a project called "Extending *Mister Rogers' Neighborhood* to Child Care," PBS stations work with early childhood educators to use the series as a training program for childcare providers.

In a study conducted by Dr. Suzanne McFarland, professor of early childhood education at the University of Toledo, 29 teachers in childcare centers around Toledo participated in using *Mister Rogers' Neighborhood.* According to the study, "teachers became more supportive of children's emotional and social development as a result of using *Mister Rogers' Neighborhood* on a regular basis....[They] were able to recognize and model Fred Rogers' nurturing behavior...teachers had become 'calmer,' used a lowered voice more often with children, and seemed more relaxed."

The teachers said it best. In their own words:

"I take out more time to answer questions, and I explain more to the children."

"The program gave me lots of new ideas and activities to do with my class."

"Mister Rogers keeps it so simple. Mister Rogers doesn't take things for granted, which I did. Now I notice that I do not take for granted what I think children already know."

> "You've made this day a special day by just being you.
> You are the only person like you in the whole world. And
> people can like you just because you're you."
> —*Mister Rogers to his TV audience*

What Mister Rogers Can Teach Grown-Ups

That fellow in the cardigan sweater and sneakers does have a special way of communicating with children. Parents who only remember Mister Rogers from parodies by Eddie Murphy on *Saturday Night Live* would do well to take a closer look.

For 26 years, Fred Rogers has been talking to children in a way that makes them feel good about themselves and helps them develop the critical sense of self-esteem at a young age. He teaches them important emotional skills to help them grow in this often inhospitable world, such as honesty, cooperation, patience, and coping with anger and disappointment.

Whether he's learning about the cello from Yo-Yo Ma or ballet from former Pittsburgh Steeler Lynn Swann, Mister Rogers models a healthy curiosity about the world. We adults could learn something from the respect and courtesy he accords each of his TV visitors. And adults who are quick to raise their voices with children could certainly benefit from watching his soft-spoken and affectionate style.

One mother, Molly, explains what she and her son learn from the program:

> One reason I love Mister Rogers is that he's so in touch with the
> child's way of seeing and experiencing the world. It's the way he

uses the medium. Everything is done in real time, there's no jumping back and forth, no quick cuts. He always uses the little train before and after the Land of Make Believe, to show that we're going to a different place.

Once, he made musical instruments out of Coke bottles and dropped blue dye in the water. The camera went in for a closeup and Mr. Rogers said, "Isn't that beautiful!" There were a few moments of silence. That's so different from the frenetic pace of children's entertainment.

And he takes the time to put things away, back on the shelf. Thank you, Mister Rogers! You're modeling putting your toys away. When he goes to a graham cracker factory to show how things are made, he models good manners, in the way he greets people. Children should be given models worthy of imitating, and Mister Rogers is a wonderful model.

Saying Good-bye to a Cat with Mister Rogers' Help

Fred Rogers has also tackled difficult topics on his program, such as divorce and death. The shows, together with his books for children, help parents learn how to talk about these seemingly "adult" topics with preschoolers.

Our cat, Beatrice, died two years ago. Maggie and Beatrice had been very close and used to curl up together in bed at night. How do you explain death to a five-year-old? I was at a loss.

Ruth and I turned to Fred Rogers' book, *When a Pet Dies*. The pet on the book cover happens to be a cat, a gray tabby just like Beatrice. In Mister Rogers' inimitable voice, the book deals with the questions kids are most likely to ask, such as "What is dying?" ("That's something everyone wonders about") and "Is it

The "Hidden Curriculum" of *Barney & Friends*

Parents whose kids are boogying with Barney might want to get to know him better. He's actually a pretty "deep" dinosaur. Drs. Jerome and Dorothy Singer, child development experts from Yale University, have analyzed the "hidden curriculum" of 48 *Barney & Friends* episodes and concluded that the show is "nearly a model for what a preschool program should be." The program addresses six major goal areas they would prescribe for preschool education:

1. **Cognitive Skills:** Introducing new vocabulary, letters, numbers, color, shapes, sorting, and sequencing skills
2. **Emotional Awareness:** Expressing joy, approval, surprise, anger, fear, and so on
3. **Social Skills:** Modeling sharing, taking turns, cooperating, helping others, and exercising self-control
4. **Physical Skills:** Demonstrating motor skills, coordination, nutrition, and health
5. **Music and Entertainment:** Singing, dancing, and playing
6. **Multicultural Exposure:** Presenting the people, language, customs, food, songs, and dances of different ethnic groups

A second study with over 100 three- and four-year-olds found that viewing *Barney & Friends* resulted in learning gains in areas of number skills, knowledge of colors and shapes, vocabulary, neighborhood locations, good manners, nature, and health. When preschool teachers reinforced the lessons, the children learned even more. And when Barney and his friends learn about autumn or make self-portraits, you can extend these activities into your home, too.

like going to sleep?" ("A pet that dies stops breathing and moving. It doesn't see or hear anymore. And it doesn't need to eat anymore.")

Mister Rogers emphasizes the importance of talking about your feelings of sadness and anger with someone who shares them. He reassures kids that "there will come a time when your sadness and anger have gone away...a time when you can feel happy again about the good times you and your pet had together."

The book encouraged us to have a family funeral for Beatrice and to involve Maggie in helping to bury her cat. She picked out a blanket to wrap Bea in, some toys to place in the cardboard box casket, and a gravestone to mark the spot in our small garden.

We found other fine children's books on the topic of death and grieving, such as Judith Viorst's *The Tenth Good Thing About Barney* (another cat), *The Two of Them* by Aliki (a daughter and her grandfather), and a *Reading Rainbow* book, *Everett Anderson's Goodbye* by Lucille Clifton (a boy and his father). In the two years since Bea died, Maggie has lost her two grandfathers and a great-grandmother. Each time, she seems to have grown more resilient. Death has become a sad and unfortunate part of her life as a child, but it has not been dark, lonely, or fearful.

Take a look at the Resource Guide for information on Mister Rogers' videos and books, on such varied topics as moving to a new neighborhood, the birth of a younger sibling, and going to the doctor, daycare center, or hospital. As he has been for me, I think you'll find Mister Rogers an unexpected tutor in learning that "special language" for talking to your child.

BOOKS AND TV CAN GO HAND IN HAND

Many people mistakenly believe that TV is the enemy of reading. Of course, it can be: A child who spends 40 hours a week in front of the set has precious little time for anything else. But there are specific programs that can actually encourage a love of reading in your child.

First, we have to let go of some old ideas about what reading is and how we learn it. The Dick-and-Jane readers we used as kids were dedicated to teaching phonics, to matching the right sounds to the right combinations of letters. Many parents still believe this is what reading is all about and invest in high-priced kits of phonics materials.

Phonics is part of the reading game but not the whole game. In fact, most children learn their phonics pretty well, even though the English language is a hazardous maze of irregular spellings and arbitrary pronunciations. That the "sh" sound is spelled variously in *shove*, *sugar*, *ocean*, and *motion* is enough to make any young reader *nauseous*. But most kids have more difficulty in comprehending the words they pronounce and using language productively in their own writing and speaking than in reading phonetically.

There is a more stimulating way for your child to experience the joys and satisfaction of reading. Most reading experts have incorporated phonics skills into the broader language arts, which include reading, writing, listening, and speaking.

Many school districts have embraced this approach to the language arts, which uses children's literature to present stories, myths, humor, characters, and a much richer use of imagery and language than found in basal readers.

Turning Off the TV, Turning to a Book

You can encourage this well-rounded approach to language skills by reading books with your child and by selectively turning on the TV. Several TV shows can serve as storytellers for your children, such as *Long Ago and Far Away* on PBS, *Madeline*, based on Ludwig Bemelmans' books, or *The World of Peter Rabbit and Friends*, both on the Family Channel.

My favorite is PBS's *Reading Rainbow*. Hosted by LeVar Burton, the program presents the best children's stories, read by celebrities such as Ed Asner and Candice Bergen, and connects them to real-life experiences through mini-documentary segments. The series has won an Emmy Award for best children's series as well as numerous other awards.

Reading Rainbow is an excellent resource for parents who want to introduce their children to different cultures and customs.

There are stories from Africa (*Knots on a Counting Rope*), Asia (*The Paper Crane*), and Native American cultures (*The Legend of the Indian Paintbrush*).

The series also presents science books and concepts. For instance, one program features the book *The Milkmakers*, takes viewers on a field trip to a dairy farm, and examines the process of cheese-making.

Teachers in the elementary grades find *Reading Rainbow* fits perfectly with their teaching of the language arts through children's literature. Now the series is the most widely used instructional TV show in the country. According to a 1992 survey by the Corporation for Public Broadcasting, more than 132,000 teachers used *Reading Rainbow* with 4.2 million students. In addition, millions of children watch it at home as well and request the books they see on the program.

Reading Rainbow is a telling example of how quality children's TV can "crossover" and motivate kids' learning in a number of settings—in the home, school, after-school program, or library.

Publishers Learned a Lesson from *Reading Rainbow*

Publishers have also learned the value of *Reading Rainbow*. Dr. Twila Liggett, the series' co-executive producer, says that initially publishers were reluctant to allow their books to be featured. "They'd say to me, 'Why would a child want to read our books when they've just seen it on TV?'" Now, the sales of *Reading Rainbow* books soar between two and 10 times as high as other books without the benefit of national TV exposure.

Well-produced series—*Ghostwriter, Square One TV,* the *National Geographic Special* programs, and *NOVA*—exploit the medium to its greatest advantage, with vivid imagery, compelling personalities, and the human interest element inherent in their subjects. Those qualities make for good learning materials, wherever the learner is located.

What to Do When Reading Rainbow Is Over

"*Reading Rainbow* gets kids to turn off the TV and turn to a book," says Dr. Twila Liggett, the show's co-executive producer. Here are some of her suggestions to encourage your kids' growing literacy skills and interests:

- **Find the *Reading Rainbow* books.** Many children's librarians and teachers designate *Reading Rainbow* books or keep a list.
- **Watch together.** An episode can inspire children to do a wide variety of literacy-building activities, such as reading, playing word games, leaving notes for each other, or writing and reading their own stories aloud. For example, after watching the episode "Eric and Flo Take the Cake," your children will see that even cooking involves reading, whether you're following a complicated recipe or the instructions on a box of cake mix.
- **Read together.** Share books and share reading time. When kids see their parents reading, they value books more, too.
- **Support reading by talking and listening.** When a child talks about her day, verbalizes her feelings, asks questions, and ponders answers, she is also increasing her literacy skills.

IT'S NOT EASY BEING GREEN AND OTHER LESSONS IN MULTICULTURAL UNDERSTANDING

Many parents we interviewed for the KQED Parents Project spoke of their goal of helping children understand the diversity of peoples and cultures in Northern California, the US, and the rest of the world. These families understood that helping children appreciate human diversity is socially responsible, intellectually interesting, and spiritually rewarding.

Yet television's influence in this area can be a double-edged sword. It can be a force for portraying the diversity and talent of many races and cultures, but it can also promote stereotyping and prejudice. For example, the Asian-Americans I know are law-abiding citizens who care about their families and their communities. Yet the most visibility we've had on the local news is as illegal aliens or kidnappers and murderers involved in some furtive gang warfare.

Racial and cultural understanding are the most important gifts we can give to our children. When society presents so many messages about racial strife, as well as overt and covert stereotypes, parents are often the first and last line of defense for combating prejudice and stereotypes.

Appreciating and celebrating racial differences start at home. And many studies point to the home as the main incubator for racial attitudes, which develop early and are remarkably resistant to change.

We're Different, We're the Same

Since 1990, *Sesame Street* has been pioneering a new approach to teach preschoolers about race. The show's innovative race relations curriculum includes special segments on African-Americans, Native Americans, Hispanic-Americans, and Asian-Americans. The program's approach to race relations can help all parents interested in raising children who appreciate diversity.

Sesame Street has always been a model in presenting a multicultural cast, young and old, who are good friends and respect each other's racial backgrounds. But the show never explicitly delved into race and racial differences. As many parents feel, it can be hard to know what to say. We are often hobbled by our own level of understanding of different races and cultures.

The *Sesame Street* staff learned that subtlety is often lost on preschoolers, such as Kermit the Frog's well-known song "Being Green." While Kermit starts off lamenting that green is not a very jazzy color, he ends up proud that green is the color of spring, big like an ocean, and tall like a tree. Though adults find the song meaningful, the slow ballad sent mixed messages to children. Some kids carried away the message that "Kermit was sad because he's green."

Such findings encouraged the *Sesame Street* writers and producers to write a more explicit curriculum about the physical differences between people, not as a way of creating categories but as a way of erasing them. They devised clear goals for the new race relations curriculum, such as "Children will learn that all skin colors, hair textures, and eye shapes are good," and "It is good for people to try new cultural and language experiences." The show encourages children to become friends with those who have a different skin color. These curriculum goals are emphasized in a new outreach program, the *Sesame Street* Preschool Education Program, which provides training to childcare providers in whose care the majority of preschoolers are now found.

A Cast of Many Colors

People aren't really white, black, or yellow. In one of the new segments, several Muppets discuss how skin colors are really more accurately called beigish-pink or tannish-brown or brownish-black. Characters point to the color of their skin with pride, as Elmo says to Whoopi Goldberg, "I like my red fur." She responds, "I like my brown skin."

Another segment celebrates the diversity of hair texture— curly, straight, kinky, thin, thick—that cuts across racial boundaries. These segments on physical characteristics are complemented by others celebrating the cultures, histories, foods, and music of different groups.

The staff also found that, while the preschoolers said they wanted to play with children from different races, their parents, carrying their adult "racial baggage," were somewhat more reluctant to let them. Some of the most effective segments feature a child of one race inviting a child of another to play a game from his culture, such as an African-American boy who invites a Caucasian boy to learn kapoeira, a martial art. In another segment, Olivia, a Caucasian girl, spends a night at the home of Ieshia, an African-American girl. They learn that their families are more similar than different.

> "One episode of *Reading Rainbow* focused on Native American stories. A segment on New Mexican pottery showed women preparing the clay and making pots. After that, my son was totally into pottery. We've signed up for a clay class that we can do together. It's a natural example of using TV to get exposure to things we couldn't do in our own home."
>
> —Molly, *mother of a son, 4*

Finding Yourself and Others on Screen

It is rare to find an Asian-American featured in a national TV series, whether drama, sitcom, or a children's program. Fortunately, some quality children's programs feature Asian-American characters in nonstereotypic roles. And public television children's programming continues to promise to show our children a wide diversity of people in positive, realistic situations, whether they be people with disabilities, from different parts of the world, or of different classes, ethnicities, or races.

Since my own daughter began calling herself a Chinese-American, around the age of four, she has been drawn to watching these other Asian-American kids on TV. Tina, the young Vietnamese-American girl on *Ghostwriter*, and Min, the Asian girl on *Barney & Friends*, have been two of her favorite characters. Maggie will point out Asian faces on TV ads, and she excitedly called me into the room when she saw the actress who plays Tina in a Nickelodeon ad about prejudice. She is proud of being Chinese and is interested in learning about Chinese customs.

Just as Maggie is interested in seeing herself and her race reflected on the TV screen, other children of color are likewise gratified to see people, especially young people, similar to them in the shows they watch. Adults are no different, as consistently borne out in Nielsen ratings. The top-ranked network programs among African-Americans were those with African-Americans in lead roles: *Fresh Prince of Bel Air*, *Roc*, *Martin*, and *In Living Color*. Our audience research for *3-2-1 Contact*, the science series, found that the young, black cast members were more popular with black children and the Hispanic cast members were more favored by Hispanic children.

TV Tips for Teaching Multiculturalism

You can use TV to encourage your child's racial and cultural understanding:

• **In your Family TV Diet, select educational children's and family programs with multiracial casts and themes.** Look especially for shows in which cultures and talents of individuals from different races are emphasized. For instance, many programs in *Reading Rainbow* feature multiethnic stories.

Ghostwriter's young, multiracial cast has a passion for communicating and solving problems using reading and writing. Several programs reflect the cultural practices from the cast members' families, who came from Vietnam or Mexico.

• **Weave learning webs with these programs and other resources.** Use these programs, together with discussions, book reading, cooking, crafts, and museum visits, to feature multicultural themes in your family's activities. These shows can be tied to school assignments your child may receive around cultural holidays. The children's librarian at your public library can provide a wealth of resources and multicultural book lists.

• **Take your lead from *Sesame Street*'s approach to race.** Instead of focusing on "adult categories" of Caucasian, African-American, Asian-American, or Latino, encourage your child to take a closer look at people's real shade of skin, shape of eye, and texture of hair. Even within one family, parents and children can discuss the diversity of colors of their own skin, eyes, and hair and extend this discussion to other families and other races, without using adult racial labels. For preschoolers, *Mister Rogers' Neighborhood* also offers many segments teaching cultural and racial diversity.

START WITH THINGS THAT WIGGLE: TV AND SCIENCE EDUCATION

Television is a wonderful, exciting window on the world of science. The TV camera can present an astonishing variety of scientific phenomena, in images and language understandable to your child. Thanks to your tax dollars, the National Science Foundation (NSF) has invested heavily in the production of the best children's programs on science, mathematics, and technology. So use them!

From 1987 through 1990, NSF spent more than $25 million on TV science series, especially on children's programs such as *3-2-1 Contact, Square One TV, Futures with Jaime Escalante,* and science programs in the *Reading Rainbow* series. Another major series based on the popular children's books, *The Magic School Bus,* takes children on animated "incredible voyages" through the solar system, volcanoes, and the digestive system. Look for other children's science programs, such as CBS's *Beakman's World,* ABC's

Cro, Bill Nye, the Science Guy on PBS and commercial stations, or the many documentaries on the Discovery Channel or other cable channels. These shows can be interwoven with related children's books and, if your community has them, stimulating visits to zoos, science centers, planetariums, and nature preserves.

Becoming a Partner in Your Child's Science Learning

Unfortunately, many parents do not make science a priority for their children, or they confine science to being a "school subject," especially if they're not confident about their own science knowledge. Many assume that science consists of memorizing the dusty facts we were taught in school, rather than real, hands-on experiences. Science programs can give parents a chance to rediscover science as well.

We need to look beyond what we've been taught about science. Science is not just about learning facts. It is about asking questions, investigating and gathering information, and thinking critically. Most importantly, it's about curiosity.

As with all learning, you don't have to know all the answers. It is more important that you share fascination and interest with science and embark on a learning adventure together with your child.

Our family has used television as part of "learning webs" in science for several years. Many times we've read a *Magic School Bus* book to Maggie about how rainwater is purified before it gets to our tap. Together we've watched a *Reading Rainbow* program that explained thunderstorms, and one in which James Earl Jones read *Bringing the Rain to Kapiti Plain*, about an African boy who brings rain to his dry pastures. We've also found how easy it is to cross the lines between science, culture, and history.

Recently, we learned more about the water cycle on a class field trip to a new sewage treatment plant. I'm learning right along with Maggie about such important environmental topics as where our water comes from, how it's cleaned, how we use it, and how precious it really is.

> "If you are looking for ways to catch the close attention of children...show them, for starters, a small bird or a monarch butterfly or a nest of mealworms. To teach science, and to want to learn science, you have to have in mind some questions beyond answering, questions that raise other questions. Television is made for this kind of display...carrying the mind down to the deepest and smallest parts of nature, and out to the farthest reaches of the cosmos. But it should start with things that wiggle."
> —*Dr. Lewis Thomas, scientist, author, and former chancellor, Memorial Sloan-Kettering Cancer Center, New York*

First Exposures to Science

In our research for the CTW series, *3-2-1 Contact*, one finding that amazed us was how little exposure children have to the scientific world, even to the most obvious sights and sounds in their own backyards. A San Francisco high school teacher once told me that some of his students have never traveled five miles to see the ocean. Unless teachers and parents make stronger efforts to expose children to the natural and technological world, we run the risk of raising a generation of scientific illiterates.

A well-designed TV series can help. *3-2-1 Contact* uses mini-documentaries to take children to scientific sites around the country and around the world, from labs where running shoes are tested to the Australian Barrier Reef to the inner chamber of a termite mound. Here are some of the things that fourth-, fifth-, and sixth-graders said they first learned from watching *3-2-1 Contact*:

> "When I fly to LA, I sit by the propeller and the wing and I notice how big those are. Now I notice how they shape it, the arch in there to create the lift. I didn't know that before *3-2-1 Contact*."
>
> "We all have a different DNA. That's what makes our voices and our eyes different and our face, our hair."
>
> "I learned that a hummingbird beats its wings 60 times a second and a bee flaps its wings 80 or 90 times a second."
>
> "I never thought termites lived in sand or mud. I always thought they lived in wood. They have all these tunnels and they build these big things. I didn't know that at all."

Parents can capitalize on another major finding from the program—that children want to learn more about what they see. Viewers not only wanted to read books on the various subjects, but also wanted to make things, such as a model volcano, a car made out of dominos, or a boomerang like ones they saw in the show. And they had lots of questions about topics they had seen: Can you clone a person? How does a microscopic camera see inside a mother's uterus? Was Lucy, the prehistoric woman, real?

These are great topics for further exploration, in books, at the library, at the science museum, and via other TV programs. You might consider helping your child with a science fair project in which a video sparked your child's questions or helped answer others.

Perhaps most importantly, the series appeared to help children to go beyond the stereotype of science as men in white lab coats pouring beakers of chemicals. As a 10-year-old girl said, "I didn't know that so much could be science. Now that I've seen all these things, I think there are so many things you could do in science and you wouldn't even think it was science!"

> "Science shows for children...have been some of the most outstanding and critically acclaimed in the history of the medium. From Don Herbert's *Mr. Wizard* in my youth to the excellent PBS series *3-2-1 Contact* by the Children's Television Workshop, TV science programs for youngsters best fulfill my own ideal for the kind of television I want my children to watch. These programs inform and intrigue young people, make them ask questions of their own, and absorb them in the mysteries of the Earth and our universe....But most important, they treat children as people, as inquiring individuals who are creative, imaginative, and capable of thinking and understanding.
> —*Vice President Al Gore, Jr.*

Science for All Ages

Another PBS series for adolescents, *Futures*, produced by FASE Productions in Los Angeles, presents science careers and information. The success of the series also demonstrates how a TV series can help stem the tide in declining science interest. Hosted by math teacher Jaime Escalante, whose teaching success was dramatized in the movie *Stand and Deliver*, it makes a pointed effort to profile people of color using math and science in careers, from airplane pilots and satellite engineers to skateboard and clothing designers.

An evaluation conducted with 12- to 14-year-olds found that viewers of the series more often agreed with statements such as "Careers that use math can be creative." The study also indicated that the series was especially appealing to African- and Hispanic-American teens, who often do not look upon science as an interest or a potential career.

"DAD, ARE YOU A VIRGIN?":
TV AND SEX EDUCATION

I was reading a bedtime story from *Ranger Rick* magazine to Maggie. Boomer Badger didn't want to help the other forest animals celebrate National Wildlife Week because he thought their theme of pollution was boring. "What a wiener of a Wildlife Week," he grumbled, as he stomped off.

Maggie started giggling and I had a feeling she wasn't thinking about frankfurters. I asked her, "What does 'wiener' mean?" She said, in between giggles, "Well, it could be a hot dog. Or it could be a penis."

The sex education of our children starts early, from a preschooler's learning to name his own body parts to his first question about "Where do babies come from?" My wife and I have learned that, although we haven't been shy about naming the private parts of our bodies, we can't control what other kids call those parts on the playground.

Yes, it's true that my daughter recently asked me whether I was a virgin. We are still working on what she means by that word. So far, she says she doesn't want to tell me. It's certainly not a word Ruth or I taught her. I find it startling that I am even having this conversation with a first-grader.

Sex is one of the most difficult topics parents can talk about with their children. It is fraught with anxiety for most of us and conjures up memories of our own sex educations, which were usually not very satisfactory. At one of our KQED focus groups with parents, a father said, "It would really be helpful to have a video about how I can talk to my son about sex. He's eight years old now, and he's beginning to ask questions about girls and sex. My wife and I are uncomfortable with the subject, and we'd like some advice."

Everything Your Kids Ever Wanted to Know... but You Were Afraid to Answer

It is tough enough fielding kids' questions about the sexual portrayals they see on TV programs and commercials. Though these scenes do provide some teachable moments and the opportunity to defuse some stereotypes (see page 67), honestly discussing sex with children is awkward, to say the least. Yet most responsible parents would rather have this information come from them than from the streets.

Fortunately, a groundbreaking and courageous program has been produced by the Children's Television Workshop, entitled *What Kids Want to Know About Sex and Growing Up*. This one-hour program, first shown on PBS in 1992, is intended to be viewed by parents and children together. In it, Rhonda Wise and Robert Selverstone, two thoughtful and experienced sex educators, answer questions from separate groups of adolescent girls and boys. They also offer direct answers to questions about safe sex, AIDS, condoms, and homosexuality. In addition, simple animated and short films explain human anatomy, intercourse, and conception.

Wise talks with the girls about changes occurring during puberty and how they feel about these changes. She answers their questions about menstruation and reassures them of the normalcy of these changes. Selverstone talks with the boys about the ways their bodies are changing, in their voices, body hair, and genitals. He answers their candid questions about erections and wet dreams. In another segment, he discusses parents' questions, uncertainties, and anxieties.

The program is recommended for parents of children ages 10 and up, but I recommend that every parent take a look at it before your children start asking. As Selverstone says, "The world today doesn't pay attention to when we want to be sex educators....We need to reclaim our rights and obligations as our children's own sexuality educators and I would suggest we do it...earlier than we are comfortable." (See the Resource Guide for video information.)

A related video by the same producers, *Brainstorm: The Truth About Your Brain on Drugs,* addresses another difficult topic for parents and their young adolescents. This video should also be required viewing for parents raising kids today.

PART V

Looking Down

the Information

Superhighway

"IT'S STILL THE CONTENT, STUPID!"

During the past few years, we have been bombarded with media hype about the "information superhighway" reaching our homes, about mergers and acquisitions between cable and phone companies and Home Shopping Networks to come, with a still undefined promise of "interactivity."

As channel capacity expands, TV is becoming less of a mass medium and more of a special-interest one. There are channels for those who love politics, science, comedy, cooking, or shopping. There are also channels in Spanish, Chinese, and other languages.

Still, no single channel fully serves the educational and informational needs of children across the age range. Public television often finds itself in a bind for airtime, when its children's shows must compete for the same time slots as adult programming. Nickelodeon, while offering some programs with positive themes, is dedicated to maximizing audience size and revenues.

167

It is too early in the next technological revolution to see whether educational channels devoted to children will emerge, since their commercial viability is uncertain and public funding seems doubtful. It's more likely that an advertiser-supported parenting channel will be developed, offering programs, products, and services for parents who are coping with contemporary parenting issues, such as having children later in life, or managing the dual stresses of parenting and a career.

Shop Around the Clock Tonight

We are at an important crossroads in our communications environment. As we approach the twenty-first century, decisions made by government, industry, public-interest groups, and others will lay the blueprint for how well these new channels and interactive services will serve our youth.

If the past is any prologue to the future, the lanes on this new highway will be clogged with companies selling products through advertising on programmed channels and on dedicated shopping channels. Phone lines will be open 24 hours, ready to take your call. It'll be even easier to shop till you drop and to watch the movie of your choice on demand.

Programs will continue to blur the lines between program content and product-selling. For example, a computer channel has been announced, which will provide computer users with the latest information on computer technology—and offer hardware, software, and services for sale.

In the midst of this new gold rush to commercialize the new media, educational and public interests may again become lost in the fray. I, along with many other public and private organizations, endorse the concept that Congress and regulators should build a "public right-of-way" on this new superhighway to meet the educational needs of children and adults.

Commercial companies who profit from the use of public property—such as our airwaves and utilities—should help fund these new public telecommunications services. In new licensing and regulatory schemes, noncommercial channels should be able to reap the full value of their services to the public. Among homes in which public television is viewed, only about one in 10 voluntarily help to support it.

Does Anyone Have Time for This?

With many more channels, will millions of Americans be spending even more hours in front of their TV sets? In the past 10 years, with the expansion of cable channels, we've gone from an average of 10 to an average of 40 channels in American homes.

Despite the quadrupling of channels in our homes, the increased choice of programs has not affected the number of hours we use TV, which has remained constant—and already substantial—at about seven hours a day from 1981 to 1993. It is unlikely that new channels will attract eight, nine, or 10 hours of viewing a day.

Once you factor in time spent working, sleeping, and eating, those hours simply don't exist. If anything, Americans are working even longer hours to make ends meet. As parents know too well, allocating our time has become a zero-sum game. To be a parent and spend time with your kids, you have to give up something—TV-watching, movie-going, book reading, socializing. Any new channels will still have to compete for their share of the seven-hour pie.

Brave New World?

In this final section, I'll take a brief look at other video and computer technologies besides TV and videocassettes that are forming part of the Information Future in our families. Should we welcome this brave new world with open arms (keeping a hand on our wallets), or should we start boarding up our information windows?

More than 50 years ago, E. B. White asked the same question about television. In 1938, he asked whether TV would be a "saving radiance in the sky" or some "new and unbearable

---

Coming Soon to a Screen Near You?

Robert Siegel, co-host of National Public Radio's *All Things Considered,* offers these suggestions for channels in the new "500 channel universe":
- The Random Access Doogie Howser Repeat Channel
- Home Shopping Network's Greatest Hits
- The Bank Robbery Channel ("the ultimate in reality-based television; real-time transmissions from bank security cameras")
- The Team Lawnmowing Channel

NPR listeners contributed a few choice channels of their own:
- FLEA-SPAN, from the American Kennel Club
- SPAM-SPAN, the canned meat channel
- C-SPAN RUN, for beginning readers in the video age
- The *Wizard of Oz* Channel, or "Auntie-Em-TV"
- Reruns of British shows on public TV on "The English Channel"

disturbance of the general peace." We can safely say now that TV has been both. But its report card contains more C's, D's, and F's than A's and B's. TV has been an underachiever, especially in the area of children's television.

We can also safely predict that the new media will be both a blessing and a curse. How much of either will depend on how they are designed, what types of information, entertainment, or educational programs and services they offer, and how those services are used by ordinary individuals like ourselves. Whether old or new media, "It's still the content, stupid!"

When it comes to new technologies, I'm not a Luddite. While I am not the first person to rush out and buy every new black box, I'm not far behind, especially when the machine offers a new and valuable service. Our home has two adults, a child, a bird, three computers, a laser printer, a modem, two TV sets, cable TV, a VCR, a camcorder, three Walkmans, a microwave, and an answering machine.

However, we are slower to acquire devices that only improve what we already have. For instance, we don't have a car phone, and we just got a CD player. I do wear a digital watch with four tiny dials that sweep out 15-second intervals each minute. This feature is totally useless. It's a reminder to me that not everything technology can do ought to be done.

THE PERSONAL COMPUTER: A TOOL FOR LEARNING

Personal computers have been in homes for more than a decade now. *Time* even voted the PC its "Person of the Year" in 1983. Yet even though the computer was heralded as a major force for education and entertainment in the home, it is still catching up to its advance press. Currently, estimates indicate around 30 percent of American homes have computers. Adults mainly use home computers to do work.

Children are also using computers—for their homework, especially writing assignments, and for fun. The computer can be an important tool for a child's learning, starting in the later preschool and early school years. It is amazing how young children quickly learn to insert a disk, open a file, type text, change fonts, create images, and click and drag a mouse. Educational computer games can become an important part of your child's "home learning hours."

Maggie started using a computer as a preschooler and now uses programs such as Kid Pix, Number Maze, and Reader Rabbit. Like many children her age, a personal computer has been part of her home since she was born. Only a generation ago, a computer with the same power filled an entire room and could only be used by scientists.

Powerful Desktop Learning Tools

The newer, more powerful computers promise to make learning even more compelling and interactive. Some CD-ROM programs combine moving video with sound and text, for instance, in an electronic encyclopedia. In the future, we will begin to see the computer as a machine combining features of all previous media—the book, the newspaper, the magazine, the television, the radio, and the VCR. The media are converging into one integrated system.

Unlike television, the computer has enjoyed a reputation as an educational technology. Most people believe that computers are good for kids and that they can learn important skills from them.

But look closely at the content of computer programs. Some are quite innovative in using characters, graphics, sound, and storyline to convey educational content. Others are nothing more than computerized flash cards or contain subtle and not-so-subtle messages about violence and sexism. Sound familiar?

Here are a few suggestions for helping your child use the computer to maximum advantage:

• **Locate programs with good content.** Find educational software programs that convey real educational value, along with attractive and challenging graphics and interactivity. Don't stick to programs that merely offer phonics or arithmetic drills, but find programs that allow your child to express her own writing, help her to see patterns, or solve problems using numbers.

For older children, creative programs enable users to conduct scientific measurements or simulate the management of a city. If you already use a database or spreadsheet program on your home computer, you might consider helping your child create a database and mailing list of his friends and relatives, or a budget of his own spending. Your child can use a simple desktop publishing program to design a class newsletter or school newspaper.

Look for reviews of children's educational software in parent publications or computer magazines. For school-age children, a computer technology coordinator in your school or school district can be a valuable source of advice. Knowledgeable sales staff in computer software stores can also provide guidance.

• **Make something for someone.** Whether children use a computer to write a letter, make a birthday card, or send a get-well message to a friend, their learning is more valuable when it serves some real purpose. Computers should be used for more than just games children play. Children can use the technology to accomplish real-life tasks.

• **Find out how a computer works.** With every new appliance in our homes and workplaces, we are becoming less and less knowledgeable about how they work. Look for a good children's encyclopedia or book that explains, through illustrations and text, how a computer works. For that matter, you might also look up how a TV, a VCR, and a videocassette work.

Cover basic points, such as the difference between hardware and software. Take apart a damaged disk and show it to your child. How much text can one disk hold? (Hint: about two books the size of this one.) A children's encyclopedia can be one of the best resources on your child's bookshelf, for answers to the many times your child asks, "How does that work?"

"I Thought You Just Turned the Key!"

Our children are growing up in an automatic world, where incredible things happen when they press a button on a microwave or a Walkman. But they, and we, rarely stop to ask how it all works.

During our research for *3-2-1 Contact*, we showed kids a segment on how the shape of an airplane wing helps create lift. A 10-year-old boy told me it was the first time he had really thought about how an airplane flew. He said, somewhat sheepishly, "I thought you just turned the key and the plane went up!"

Unless parents and teachers make stronger efforts to explain this complex world to our children, it will be no wonder if many of them grow up intellectually complacent. It would be ironic and tragic if this generation of children grew up computer-literate but scientifically illiterate. These sorts of investigations into "how things work" can be excellent home learning projects, perfect for school assignments and science fairs—and for learning right along with your child. Haven't you ever wondered how a fax machine works, anyway?

VIDEO GAMES: ARE THE MARIO BROTHERS REALLY SO SUPER?

Video games aren't just joysticks and buttons. The technology is the same as personal computers—and you could play the same games, with the same graphics and sound, using a mouse and a keyboard. The distinction is not one of hardware, but of software. It's the contents of video games that make us think about them differently from computers or television.

Video games have been around since the 1970s. Remember the simple table tennis game of Pong, where a ball was bounced from paddle to paddle, or later, Pac-Man? As sound and graphics improved and the art of game design developed, video game consoles proliferated in video arcades, shopping centers, movie theaters, and, thanks to Sega and Nintendo, our living rooms.

The video game industry, after some fits and starts in the early 1980s, has become a huge business. In 1990, it was a $4 billion industry, a dominant portion of the toy industry. In 1989, 25 of the 30 best-selling toys in America were video games or equipment. According to the Electronic Industries Association and A. C. Nielsen, as of January 1994, video game players were present in 42 percent of American homes, a higher figure than for home computers (30 percent) or camcorders (21 percent).

The Boy Toys

While Sega and Nintendo have published some educational games, such as *Sesame Street* ones, the video game industry has been overwhelmingly commercial, devoted to games that use action/adventure themes. Action films play a big part in these games: There are video games based on many films, such as *Robo-Cop*, *Teenage Mutant Ninja Turtles*, *Predator*, and *Platoon*. Not surprisingly, the primary users of video games are boys.

The storylines of these games often involve physical combat, high-speed racing, and laser space wars. Some of them are sadistic and sexist, with a vengeance. In *Mortal Kombat*, the victor has the option of killing the loser by tearing out his heart, pulling out his spine, or decapitating him. In the sexually explicit *Night Trap*, three men in black masks burst into the bedroom of a woman dressed in a negligee, drag her off, and hold her down while a fourth attacker plunges an electric drill into her neck. Several senators and members of Congress, representing the public's outrage, have introduced bills in Congress to develop ratings systems on video game packages.

Dr. Eugene Provenzo, of the School of Education at the University of Miami, interviewed kids, parents, and teachers in his thoughtful analysis of video games, their content, and their impact on kids. In his book *Video Kids: Making Sense of Nintendo*, he warns: "We need to eliminate the violence, destruction, xenophobia, racism, and sexism that are so much a part of the world of Nintendo."

Most video games have little redeeming social or educational value. Even more disturbing, Provenzo found parents lacked awareness or interest in monitoring their children's playing with the games.

Conscious parenting requires parents who know content. Parents *must* scrutinize the contents of each electronic box our children use in the home—whether television, computers, or video games. We cannot simply turn our backs and resign ourselves to accepting that these programs, disks, and cartridges are a part of a modern child's life. In the case of many video games, we do so at our children's peril.

> "I was just talking to a little girl right there. From three o'clock when she gets home she stays in front of that television and the video games, she doesn't play outside at all, she doesn't read for pleasure. That's her total free time occupation."
> —*Sixth-grade teacher in Eugene Provenzo's*
> Video Kids: Making Sense of Nintendo

YOUR FAMILY CAMCORDER: DEMYSTIFYING THE MEDIUM

Just about every parent I know is amazed at how quickly a child learns to point and click the remote control, easily switching channels and playing cassettes on the VCR. It is astonishing to see a two- or three-year-old using his little hands with such dexterity. At an early age, by pressing the right buttons, he's gaining a measure of control over TV that we, as children, certainly never had.

The camcorder has become an everyday appliance in many homes, enabling families to gain the ultimate control: making our own television. Our family takes the camcorder along on vacations and to family celebrations and school events. Many children now have their own video biographies, their days captured as an infant, their first baby steps, and the first day of school. As they grow up, they can relive their lives through this vivid medium, seeing and hearing their first birthdays, their first friends, and their relatives, including grandparents who may now be gone.

Starring in Your Own Life Story

Your family's camcorder can help your child complete the move from being merely a consumer of video to being a producer. Changes in video technology and lower prices now enable you and your family to have access to high-quality video cameras. As with computers, your child can now hold in her hands a complex technology used only by trained professionals a generation ago. Your child can become a producer, director, and cameraperson at the ripe old age of eight.

There are already innovative projects around the country in which video producers are placing cameras in the hands of children and teens, encouraging them to tell their own stories. If your child is of school age, you might ask your teacher or principal to have a videographer visit your child's class to do a unit on media-making. You might be willing to do this yourself.

Meanwhile, here are a few suggestions on helping your child use the camcorder:

- **Teach your child to use the camcorder.** You'll have to judge when your child is ready. I've seen many five- and six-year-old videographers, shooting videos at the zoo, with a little help from Mom and Dad. Explain the various features for recording picture and sound. Let your child shoot a video at family events, outings, or just around the house, capturing those everyday moments you'll want to look back on years from now.

Help him learn to shoot economically. A few minutes of a scene at the park or an interview with an uncle are enough. Watch the video together when you play it back and talk about the scenes he shot. He'll understand that he's doing something valued in the family, and that he's good at it. And he'll learn to look at video as something people make, helping to demystify what he sees on TV.

- **Let your child create a personal video album.** Encourage her to make a collection of her own video recordings, just as she makes photo albums of pictures she has taken. Give her a blank tape, let her label it, and use it whenever she's shooting with the camcorder. With these tapes, she'll have a chronological record of her early years as a videographer.

- **Help your child understand how a camcorder works.** Get out that children's encyclopedia or "how things work" book. Take the time to explain to your child, at a level he can understand, how images and sound are recorded on videotape, and how these are played back on the VCR. With this act, you are conveying important messages: that "how things work" is worth thinking about, and that camcorders, VCRs, and computers are amazing and wondrous pieces of technology invented and made by humans.

If you have access to editing equipment or can hook up your camcorder to a VCR, you can also teach your child some simple editing, assembling the "best of" your child's work onto one cassette. Using a multimedia computer system, children are already able to create autobiographies and stories about their communities using video, audio, photos, and text. The technology for doing so will become less expensive and easier to use in the years ahead. Perhaps one benefit of the camcorder will be to help our children and ourselves reexamine our lives and even contemplate our futures.

PARENTS WILL STILL BE THE MOST IMPORTANT TEACHERS

As we all ease onto the information superhighway, I hope we'll remember where we've come from, because some things will not change. The family will still be the most important educational institution in this country, and parents will still be our children's first and most important teachers.

The new media hold the promise of bringing new educational experiences to our eyes and ears, but the public interest requires that these services be brought to all and not only to those who can afford to pay. Whether the current industry struggle over hardware and software, channels and programming, licensing and regulation will benefit the public interest remains to be seen.

Will there be a robust system of public telecommunications, extending the contributions of public broadcasting, as well as of our libraries, schools, and museums, to our nation's culture and education? Or will the new media be privatized for primarily commercial interests? If the latter proves true, we may well end up in Bruce Springsteen's nightmare—"500 channels and nothin' on."

The most important learning, though, will not come from new machines and screens but from what parents, teachers, and children do with them, together. It will be even more important to talk to our kids so they will learn, to engage in that ongoing educational dialogue, and to spend our time with them wisely.

For as channels increase and new devices multiply, one immutable fact of life will remain: There will still be just 24 hours in a day. Helping your child spend those hours productively will still be the most valuable thing you can do.

I'd like to know if you've found the ideas in this book helpful. Drop me a line about how your family uses television and the Family TV Diet, shows you and your children have learned from, what sorts of learning webs you're weaving, or other reactions to this book. You can write to me at the following address: Milton Chen, *The Smart Parent's Guide to Kids' TV,* KQED, 2601 Mariposa St., San Francisco, CA 94110.

AFTERWORD

Fred Rogers

Creator of *Mister Rogers' Neighborhood*

There's a genuine warmth at the heart of Milton Chen's writing, just as there is at the heart of the man himself. All families need such honest care—no matter what the medium.

Milton's work, like ours, has been in public television: the place on the television dial that parents have learned to trust. Parents often tell me this is so. I think they mean that public television is a place which has a genuine respect for their children as human beings with needs and feelings and growing values.

One of our favorite stories here in this Neighborhood is about a two-year-old who, after watching our visit with cellist Yo-Yo Ma, started using a chopstick for a bow on an old guitar. His mother wrote to tell us, "I've never seen anything like it. He actually cried until I told him we'd try to find some way for him to 'play the cello.' That was three years ago, and very recently we learned that that little boy is still playing the cello, and his mother has decided to learn to play, too!

Milton Chen helps parents understand that television is not just *watched*. It's swallowed…and digested. That's why we who make television for children must be especially careful with what we produce, with the people we present, and with the attitudes we show in television relationships—attitudes of respect, kindness, healthy curiosity, determination, and love, just as parents would want for their children.

Television plays such an enormous role in our children's growing up, and it is adults, first and foremost, who shape children's
values. We parents need to think hard about how television is
affecting our children and, in turn, our grandchildren to come.
We need to think harder still about what to do about it. Through
this helpful book, Milton Chen has given many clear and caring
ideas for families to consider.

REFERENCES

Action for Children's Television, Kim Hays, ed. *TV, Science & Kids: Teaching Our Kids to Question.* Reading, MA: Addison-Wesley, 1984.

Aliki. *The Two of Them.* New York: Mulberry Books, 1979.

Anderson, Daniel. "The Influence of Television on Children's Attentional Abilities." Amherst, MA: University of Massachusetts, Department of Psychology. Unpublished paper, December 1985.

Ball, Samuel, and Gerry A. Bogatz. *The First Year of Sesame Street: An Evaluation.* Princeton, NJ: Educational Testing Service, 1970.

Berenstain, Stan and Jan. *The Berenstain Bears and Too Much TV.* New York: Random House, 1984.

Berry, Gordon, and Joy Keiko Asamen. *Children & Television: Images in a Changing Sociocultural World.* Newbury Park, CA: Sage Publications, 1993.

Bloom, Benjamin, ed. *Developing Talent in Young People.* New York: Ballantine, 1985.

Bogart, Leo. "The American Media System and Its Commercial Culture." New York: Freedom Forum Media Studies Center. (Occasional Paper No. 8, March 1991, 2950 Broadway, New York, NY 10027.)

Boyer, Ernest L. *Ready to Learn: A Mandate for the Nation.* Princeton, NJ: The Carnegie Foundation for the Advancement of Teaching, 1993.

Charren, Peggy, and Martin W. Sandler. *Changing Channels: Living (Sensibly) with Television.* Reading, MA: Addison-Wesley, 1983.

Chen, Milton. "A Review of Research on the Educational Potential of *3-2-1 Contact*: A Children's TV Series on Science and Technology." New York: Children's Television Workshop, 1984. (ERIC Document Reproduction Service No. ED 265 849.)

Chen, Milton. "Television and Informal Science Education: Assessing the Past, Present, and Future of Research." In *Informal Science Learning*, edited by Valerie Crane. Dedham, MA: Research Communications Ltd., 1994.

Chen, Milton, and William Marsh. "Myths About Instructional Television: A Riposte." *Education Week* (May 24, 1989).

Children's Television Workshop. *Sesame Street Research Bibliography*. New York, 1989.

Children's Television Workshop and Educational Testing Service. *Sesame Street Research: A 20th Anniversary Symposium*. New York and Princeton, NJ, 1990.

Clifton, Lucille. *Everett Anderson's Goodbye*. New York: Henry Holt & Co., 1983.

Comer, James P. *Maggie's American Dream: The Life and Times of a Black Family*. New York: Penguin Books, 1988.

Copperman, Paul. *Taking Books to Heart: How to Develop a Love of Reading in Your Child*. Reading, MA: Addison-Wesley, 1986.

Corporation for Public Broadcasting. *Study of School Uses of Television and Video: Summary Report*. Washington, DC, 1992.

Crane, Valerie, ed. *Informal Science Learning: What Research Says About Television, Science Museums, and Community-Based Projects*. Dedham, MA: Research Communications, Ltd., 1994.

Faber, Adele, and Elaine Mazlish. *How to Talk So Kids Will Listen & Listen So Kids Will Talk*. New York: Avon Books, 1980.

Fite, Katherine V. "Television and the Brain: A Review." Amherst, MA: University of Massachusetts, 1993.

Gibbons, James, W. R. Kincheloe, and K. S. Down. "Tutored Videotape Instruction: A New Use of Electronics Media in Education." *Science* 195 (1977): 1139–1146.

Gore, Albert, Jr. "What Have They Done to You, Captain Kangaroo?"
In *Action for Children's Television, TV, Science & Kids: Teaching Our
Children to Question*, edited by Kim Hays, 116-120. Reading, MA:
Addison-Wesley, 1984.

Healy, Jane. *Endangered Minds: Why Our Children Don't Think*. New
York: Simon & Schuster, 1990.

Home, Anna. *Into the Box of Delights: A History of Children's Television*.
London: BBC Books, 1993.

Huston, Aletha C., Edward Donnerstein, et al. *Big World, Small Screen:
The Role of Television in American Society*. Lincoln, NE: University of
Nebraska Press, 1992.

Leonard, George. *Education and Ecstasy*. Berkeley, CA: North Atlantic
Books, 1986–87.

McFarland, Suzanne L.. "Extending the Neighborhood to Childcare: A
Research Report." University of Toledo, 1992.

Mielke, Keith W. "On the Relationship Between Television Viewing
and Academic Achievement." *Journal of Broadcasting and Electronic
Media*, in press.

Minow, Newton N. "How Vast the Wasteland Now?" New York: The
Freedom Forum Media Studies Center, 1991.

NFO Research, Inc. *Final Report*: Reading Rainbow *Study*. August
1990.

Nielsen Media Research. *1992–93 Report on Television*. New York,
1993.

Palmer, Edward L. *Television and America's Children*. New York:
Oxford University Press, 1988.

Postman, Neil. *Amusing Ourselves to Death*. New York: Viking Penguin, 1985.

Provenzo, Eugene F., Jr. *Video Kids: Making Sense of Nintendo*. Cam-
bridge, MA: Harvard University Press, 1991.

Reynolds, Jan. *Far North: Vanishing Cultures*. New York: Harcourt Brace Jovanovich, 1992.

RMC Research Corporation. "The Impact of *Reading Rainbow* on Libraries." Hampton, NH. 1989.

Rogers, Fred. *When a Pet Dies*. New York: G. P. Putnam and Sons, 1988.

Sallis, James F. "Promoting Healthful Diet and Physical Activity." In *Promoting the Health of Adolescents: New Directions for the 21st Century*, edited by Susan G. Millstein, Anne C. Petersen, and Elena O. Nightingale. New York: Oxford University Press, 1993.

Singer, Dorothy G. and Singer, Jerome L. "*Barney & Friends* as Education and Entertainment" Yale University, 1993.

Taras, Howard, James F. Sallis, Philip R. Nader, and Julie Nelson. "Children's Television Viewing Habits and the Family Environment." *American Journal of Diseases of Children* 144, no. 3 (March 1990): 357-359.

Television Viewing Lab. *Couch Potato Chronicles: How People Really Watch Television*. Boston: WGBH, November, 1992.

_____. *Couch Potato Chronicles: Children's Television Viewing*. Boston: WGBH, February 1994.

Thomas, Lewis. Foreword. In *TV, Science, and Kids: Teaching Our Kids to Question*, Action for Children's Television, edited by Kim Hays, ix–x. Reading, MA: Addison-Wesley, 1984.

Viorst, Judith. *The Tenth Good Thing About Barney*. New York: Macmillan, 1971.

Winn, Marie. *The Plug-In Drug: Television, Children, and the Family*. New York: Viking Penguin, 1977.

_____. *Unplugging the Plug-In Drug*. New York: Viking Penguin, 1987.

RESOURCE GUIDE

Listed below are selected organizations, print materials, and videos to help you become a more active consumer of children's television.

Center for Media Literacy
This membership organization translates media literacy research and theory into practical information and provides training and educational tools for teachers, youth leaders, parents, and caregivers of children.
1962 S. Shenandoah St.
Los Angeles, CA 90034
(800) 226-9494
Fax: (310) 559-9396

The Children and Television Project/The National Association for Family and Community Education
This nonprofit organization advocates using children's television as a learning tool for childcare centers and schools; helps parents teach children to critically interpret programming; and hosts multigenerational discussions.
PO Box 835
Burlington, KY 41005
(606) 586-8333
Fax: (606) 586-8348

The Children's Television Resource and Education Center (CTREC)
Dedicated to helping parents and teachers deal with issues related to children's TV viewing, CTREC offers print materials and educational services, such as a workshop called Helping Children Survive Television.
340 Townsend St., Suite 423
San Francisco, CA 94107
(415) 243-9943
Fax: (415) 243-9037

KIDSNET
This national, nonprofit computerized clearinghouse provides information for adults on children's audio, video, radio, and television programming. KIDSNET produces a monthly bulletin and calendar as well as
publications available in print and electronically via America OnLine
and CompuServe.

6856 Eastern Ave., NW, Suite 208
Washington, DC 10012
(202) 291-1400
Fax: (202) 882-7315
America OnLine: kidsnet@aol.com
CompuServe: 76711,1212

National Telemedia Council
Through teachers, parents, and other caregivers, this nonprofit membership organization promotes media literacy and critical television
viewing skills for youths and children via workshops and its quarterly
journal, *Telemedium*.

120 E. Wilson St.
Madison, WI 53703
(608) 257-7712
Fax: (608) 257-7714

Strategies for Media Literacy, Inc.
This national, nonprofit organization provides media literacy education
resources, workshops, and support for teachers of media in the United
States.

1095 Market St., Suite 617
San Francisco, CA 94103
(415) 621-2911

ADVOCACY GROUPS

Center for Media Education & Campaign for Kids' TV
This national organization works to ensure that the nation's children have access to quality programming. Membership includes: a quarterly newsletter featuring articles on kids and television; regular updates and action alerts on critical legislative initiatives and television industry developments affecting children; and substantial discounts on videos, booklets, and other materials regarding television and the family.
1511 K St., NW, Suite 518
Washington, DC 20005
(202) 628-2620
Fax: (202) 628-2554
Internet: cme@access.digex.net

Children's Advertising Review Unit (CARU)
A self-regulatory agency for advertisers, CARU promotes responsible children's advertising and responds to public concerns. The group reviews national child-directed advertising in all media. Brochures are available outlining these guidelines, as well as guides for parents to help their children understand the nature of advertising.
National Advertising Division
Council of Better Business Bureaus, Inc.
845 Third Ave.
New York, NY 10022
(212) 705-0123
Fax: (212) 308-4743

Coalition for Quality Children's Videos
The Coalition is committed to increasing the visibility and availability of quality children's videos. It provides education, publications, and a database of recommended video titles.
535 Cordova Rd., Suite 456
Santa Fe, NM 87501
(505) 989-8076
Fax: (505) 986-8477

National Foundation to Improve Television (NFIT)
NFIT works to reduce the amount of excessive violence shown on
television during hours when the majority of the viewing audience is
children.
60 State St., Suite 3400
Boston, MA 02109
(617) 523-6353
Fax: (617) 523-4619

NATIONAL TELEVISION NETWORKS AND ASSOCIATIONS

ABC Entertainment
2040 Avenue of the Stars
Los Angeles, CA 90067

CBS Entertainment
7800 Beverly Blvd.
Los Angeles, CA 90036

Fox Broadcasting Company
Network Division
1211 Sixth Ave.
New York, NY 10036

National Association of Broadcasters
1771 N St., NW
Washington, DC 20036

National Cable TV Association
1724 Massachusetts Ave., NW
Washington, DC 20036

NBC Entertainment
3000 W. Alameda
Burbank, CA 91523

Public Broadcasting Service
1320 Braddock Pl.
Alexandria, VA 22314-1698

Turner Broadcasting System
1 CNN Center
Atlanta, GA 30303

GOVERNMENT AGENCIES

Bureau of Consumer Protection
Federal Trade Commission
Washington, DC 20580

Federal Communications Commission
Mass Media Bureau
2025 M St., NW
Room 8210
Washington, DC 20554

United States House of Representatives
Subcommittee on Telecommunications
B-331 Rayburn Bldg.
Washington, DC 20515

United States Senate
Subcommittee on Communications
227 Hart Senate Office Bldg.
Washington, DC 20510

PRINT MATERIALS ON MEDIA LITERACY

***Cable in the Classroom* Magazine**
This magazine, geared for educators but also useful for parents, offers
detailed listings by subject of educational programming on cable. One-
year subscription: $18.
86 Elm St.
Peterborough, NH 03458
(800) 216-2225
Fax: (603) 924-6338

Media Violence and Children
This guide offers parents methods to counteract violence portrayed in
the media.
National Association for the Education of Young Children (NAEYC)
1509 Sixteenth St., NW
Washington, DC 20036-1426
(800) 424-2460
Fax: (202) 328-1846

The National PTA Catalog
This catalog includes a pamphlet entitled *Television & Your Family*,
providing tips on how to teach children and teens TV viewing skills.
Spanish publications are also available.
The National PTA
330 N. Wabash Ave., Suite 2100
Chicago, IL 60611-3690
(312) 670-6782
Fax: 670-6783

Talking with TV: A Guide to Starting Dialogue with Youth
This guide shows parents and other adults how to use entertainment
television to spark discussions with children and teens about sexuality,
race, drugs, values, responsibility, communication, and other sensitive
subjects.
Center for Population Options
1025 Vermont Ave., NW
Suite 200
Washington, DC 20005
(202) 347-5700
Fax: (202) 347-2263

10 Tips to Help Make Television a Positive Supplement to Your Child's Learning
This brochure for parents provides tips to help children become intelligent and critical viewers of television.
National Education Association
1201 Sixteenth St., NW
Washington, DC 20036
(202) 822-7216
Fax: (202) 822-7033

You Can Use Television to Stimulate Your Child's Reading Habits
To receive a free brochure, send a self-addressed, stamped envelope.
International Reading Association
800 Barksdale Rd.
PO Box 8139
Newark, DE 19714-8139
(302) 731-1600
Fax: (302) 731-1057

VIDEOS ON MEDIA LITERACY

The following videos can be ordered through VideoFinders, the video service run by Los Angeles PBS station KCET. With over 120,000 titles, VideoFinders is a great resource, particularly for educational and PBS-aired titles. To order a video, call (800) 343-4727.

Buy Me That Series
These half-hour specials coproduced by HBO and *Consumer Reports* promote children's critical consumer skills. *Buy Me That: A Kid's Survival Guide to Advertising* and its sequel, *Buy Me That, Too,* analyze the way television commercials misrepresent the toys they feature. *Buy Me That: A Kid's Survival Guide to Food Advertising* shows children how food commercials attempt to manipulate them.

On Television
A three-part series, these videos take a look at television as the nation's foremost educational institution. Titles include *Public Trust on Private Property*, *The Violence Factor*, and *Teach the Children*, which is recommended by the National PTA.

Zillions TV
Targeting six- to 13-year-olds, this half-hour special produced by Consumer Reports Television is adapted from the award-winning magazine *Zillions*. It features kids using easy to understand testing techniques to examine product claims and reveal some of the best toys and games to buy.

RELATED PRODUCTS FOR PUBLIC TV CHILDREN'S SERIES

Videos can be ordered through VideoFinders (see page 193) at (800) 343-4727. Books and audiotapes can be ordered from the following companies.

Programs for Preschoolers

Barney & Friends

Lamb Chop's Play-Along
Lamb Chop Books, such as *One Minute Bedtime Stories*, are available through:
Doubleday
666 Fifth Ave.
New York, NY 10103
(800) 223-6834

Mister Rogers' Neighborhood
For a free catalog of videos, audiocassettes, and books contact:
Family Communications
Marketing Department
4802 Fifth Ave.
Pittsburgh, PA 15213
(412) 687-2990

Sesame Street
Print materials, such as *Sesame Street Magazine* and *Parent's Guide*, are available by subscription.
Sesame Street Magazine
PO Box 52000
Boulder, CO 80322-2000
(800) 678-0613

Shining Time Station
Books, videos, plush toys, and games are available through:
Quality Family Entertainment
1133 Broadway, Suite 1520
New York, NY 10010
(212) 463-9623

Programs for School-Age Kids

Anne of Green Gables and **Anne of Avonlea** (Available through Video-Finders, page 193)

The Electric Company
Though long off the air,*The Electric Company* is one of the Children's Television Workshop's most oft-requested programs. Four videos are now being released combining new material with segments from the original show.(Available through VideoFinders, page 193)

Ghostwriter
Books are published by Bantam and are available in libraries and large bookstores.

Reading Rainbow
Books featured can be purchased at local bookstores or checked out from your local library.

3-2-1 Contact Extras
Brainstorm: The Truth About Your Brain on Drugs and *What Kids Want to Know About Sex and Growing Up*. Other videotapes, which include a free teacher's guide, covering topics such as ecology, environmental concerns, and AIDS, are available.

The author gratefully acknowledges permission to use excerpts from:

Developing Talent in Young People, ©1985 by Benjamin Bloom, Ed. Reprinted by permission of Ballantine Books, Random House, Inc.

Maggie's American Dream by James P. Comer, M.D. ©1988 by James P. Comer, M.D. Used by permission of Dutton Signet, a division of Penguin Books USA Inc.

Taking Books to Heart: How to Develop a Love of Reading in Your Child, ©1986 by Paul Copperman. Reprinted by permission of Addison-Wesley Publishing Company, Inc.

"How Vast The Wasteland Now?" ©1991 by Newton Minow. Reprinted by permission of the Freedom Forum Media Studies Center.

Brief portions of this book were adapted from an article by the author and William Marsh, titled "Myths About Instructional Television," published in the May 24, 1989, issue of *Education Week* and *Informal Science Learning*, edited by Valerie Crane and published by Research Communications Ltd. of Dedham, Massachusetts, in 1994.

INDEX

ABOUT THE AUTHOR

Milton Chen, Ph.D., brings over 20 years of experience in children's television to his role as Director of the KQED Center for Education and Lifelong Learning (CELL) in San Francisco. The Center helps learners of all ages extend their educational opportunities with public television programming and services. Among other activities, the Center provides the *Sesame Street* Preschool Educational Program (PEP) to childcare teachers and parents, and via the new Family Membership, publications and seminars to encourage greater parental involvement in children's educational television.

For the past 20 years, Dr. Chen has worked in program development, audience research, and community outreach for public television's most popular children's series, including *Sesame Street*, *The Electric Company*, *Square One TV*, and *Ghostwriter*, all produced by Children's Television Workshop (CTW) in New York. He served as Director of Research for CTW's *3-2-1 Contact*, a science and technology program for 8- to 12-year-olds, and was an assistant professor at the Harvard Graduate School of Education, where he taught and conducted research on educational media. He also serves on advisory committees for CTW, The Office of Technology Assessment for the US Congress, and Scholastic Productions, among others.

Dr. Chen has published over 20 articles and book chapters on the use of television and computers in education. His work has received awards from PBS, CTW, the American Psychological

Association, and other organizations. A graduate of Harvard College, he received his Ph.D. in communication research from Stanford University.

He lives with his wife and daughter in San Francisco.

KQED is governed by an elected, volunteer board of directors. These dedicated citizens plan the station's direction and work with the professional staff and the hundreds of thousands of loyal members to bring the highest quality television, radio, and print programming to local audiences. We gratefully salute these members of the KQED Board of Directors: Edward M. Allen, Anne C. Broome, Lyn Chan, E. Michael Darby, MD, Lois M. DeDomenico, Rosemarie Fernandez-Ruel, Stanley J. Friedman, Sasha Futran, William D. Glenn, Charlene C. Harvey (Chair), Thomas Hsieh, Jr., John H. Jacobs, Shelley A. Kessler, Henry M. Kroll, Marian E. Lever, Cynthia C. Magowan, Jerry W. Mapp, Leo P. Martinez, Robert B. Philipp, Mary Camblin Reed, Jonathan C. Rice, Sylvia M. Siegel, Kenneth H. Simmons, Sherry H. Smith, Leo C. Soong, William G. Toland III, Stephen N. Worthington.

And we recognize the dedicated contributions of the boards and staff of our 346 sister stations throughout the PBS network.

Support your local public broadcasting station!

Every community across America is reached by one of the
346 member stations of the Public Broadcasting System. These
stations bring information, entertainment, and insight for the
whole family.

Think about the programs you enjoy and remember most:

Sesame Street . . . *Ghostwriter* . . . *Reading Rainbow* . . . *Nova* . . .
Nature . . . *"I'll Fly Away"* . . . *Mystery* . . . *Masterpiece Theatre* . . .
MacNeil/Lehrer News Hour . . . *Great Performances* . . . *National
Geographic* . . . *American Playhouse* . . . and so much more.

On your local PBS station, you'll also find fascinating adult
education courses, provocative documentaries, great cooking
and do-it-yourself programs, and thoughtful local analysis.

And f[...]
a cou[...]
cable[...]ur

Help [...]
of yo[...]